Software Design Principles

A Practical Guide

Moises Gamio

ISBN: 9798848053401

DEDICATION

To Lorena.

Contents

PREFACE

This book, "Software Design Principles," delves deep into the intricate world of software design with Object-oriented programming (OOP), offering readers a comprehensive roadmap to understanding and mastering the principles that drive the creation of effective and elegant software systems. It is of vital importance to learn the fundamental concepts of object orientation before starting to translate business requirements into technical specifications and programming.

Through a rich tapestry of real-world examples, case studies, you will gain a deep understanding of fundamental design principles, such as DRY (Don't Repeat Yourself), YAGNI (You aren't going to need it), SOLID, Separation of Concerns, and others, as well as discover how they translate into tangible benefits in terms of code quality, reusability, and ease of maintenance.

This book is intended to be a timeless resource applicable across programming languages, frameworks, and domains. While programming technologies have been changing and evolving over the years, object-oriented concepts and design principles remain a constant–no matter the platform.

So, whether you are just starting your journey in software design or are a seasoned practitioner seeking to deepen your expertise, I invite you to dive into the world of software design principles. Together, we will unravel the secrets of crafting software that is not only functional but also a work of art.

codersite.dev
Moises Gamio

Introduction

Software or program design is a complex process limited only by our imagination, reasoning, opinions, and experience. To create software for commercial purposes, we must consider the abstractions and standard notations to understand and support the design process.

Software design is everything related to managing interdependencies between different software components.

Similar to what happens in network firewalls that are used to protect internal resources from intentional external attacks. In software design, these attacks come from the developers themselves, but they are not on purpose but rather the result of poor dependency management.

To protect private networks, firewalls implement sophisticated rules and policies for incoming external requests using expensive tools and hardware. In software, we need to ensure that every new developer entering a project has a minimal understanding of software design principles to protect our original design.

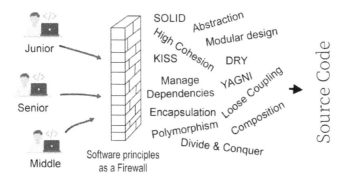

Software design principles

Don't try to achieve all software design principles from the beginning. Software design is an iterative process. At each iteration, only introduce a new design principle into your code if necessary. When changes are required, the refactoring process will be minimal.

Software is malleable, which means it is initially very flexible and subject to change. This means you should build a product that easily supports changes to your code. To facilitate these changes, adopt software design principles from the start. Communicate this idea to the rest of the members of your team.

Software Design Principles

Software design principles are guidelines and best practices that help software developers create high-quality, maintainable, and efficient software.

Let's see some commonly recognized software design principles.

Don't Repeat Yourself (DRY)

The DRY principle states that code should not be repeated unnecessarily. Instead, developers should use abstractions, modularization, and other techniques to reduce repetition and make code more maintainable.

The DRY principle also state that every piece of knowledge must have a single, unambiguous, authoritative representation within a system. The principle was formulated in the book "The Pragmatic Programmer[1]".

The principle aims to avoid the creation of duplicate representations of knowledge, which means avoiding duplicated code in our software.

For example, if you have routines where you need to format specific data, move them to a Utility interface. Create a reference to the abstract interface from different parts of your application and use its standard methods.

Creating abstractions helps to avoid code duplication. The *open-closed* and *single-responsibility* principles rely on DRY principle.

Consider using frameworks and libraries that encapsulate common logic.

Example 1: Refactoring Duplicate Code into a Method

Suppose you have the following code that calculates the area of two different rectangles in different parts of the application:

---

[1] https://en.wikipedia.org/wiki/The_Pragmatic_Programmer

```
public class AreaCalculator {
  public static void main(String[] args) {
    int width1 = 5;
    int height1 = 10;
    int area1 = width1 * height1;
    System.out.println("Area of rectangle 1: " + area1);

    int width2 = 7;
    int height2 = 3;
    int area2 = width2 * height2;
    System.out.println("Area of rectangle 2: " + area2);
  }
}
```

In this example, the formula for calculating the area (**width * height**) is duplicated. If this formula ever changes (e.g., you start considering a border area), you'd have to update it in multiple places, which could lead to errors.

Refactored Code:

```
public class AreaCalculator {
  public static void main(String[] args) {
    System.out.println("Area of rectangle 1: " + calculateArea(5, 10));
    System.out.println("Area of rectangle 2: " + calculateArea(7, 3));
  }

  private static int calculateArea(int width, int height) {
    return width * height;
  }
}
```

By moving the area calculation to a calculateArea method, we remove redundancy. Now if we need to change the calculation, we only do it in one place.

Example 2: Using Constants to Avoid Magic Numbers

Here's an example with "magic numbers," which are hardcoded values that might be used multiple times in a program.

```
public class CircleCalculator {
  public static void main(String[] args) {
    double radius1 = 5;
    double area1 = 3.14159 * radius1 * radius1;
    System.out.println("Area of circle 1: " + area1);

    double radius2 = 7;
    double area2 = 3.14159 * radius2 * radius2;
```

```
      System.out.println("Area of circle 2: " + area2);
   }
}
```

Here, `3.14159` is repeated. This not only violates DRY but also reduces code readability.

Refactored Code with Constants:

```
public class CircleCalculator {
  private static final double PI = 3.14159;

  public static void main(String[] args) {
    System.out.println("Area of circle 1: " + calculateCircleArea(5));
    System.out.println("Area of circle 2: " + calculateCircleArea(7));
  }

  private static double calculateCircleArea(double radius) {
    return PI * radius * radius;
  }
}
```

By defining `PI` as a constant, the code is cleaner, and if you ever need to change the value of `PI` (e.g., to use `Math.PI`), you can do it in one place.

Example 3: Reducing Redundancy with Inheritance

Imagine you have two classes, `Dog` and `Cat`, with similar `eat` and `sleep` methods. If you duplicate these methods in both classes, you violate the DRY principle:

```
class Dog {
  public void eat() {
    System.out.println("Dog is eating");
  }

  public void sleep() {
    System.out.println("Dog is sleeping");
  }
}
class Cat {
  public void eat() {
    System.out.println("Cat is eating");
  }

  public void sleep() {
    System.out.println("Cat is sleeping");
  }
```

```
}
```

Refactored Code Using Inheritance:

```java
class Animal {
  public void eat() {
    System.out.println("Animal is eating");
  }

  public void sleep() {
    System.out.println("Animal is sleeping");
  }
}

class Dog extends Animal {
  // Additional dog-specific behavior
}

class Cat extends Animal {
  // Additional cat-specific behavior
}
```

By moving `eat` and `sleep` methods into a common `Animal` superclass, `Dog` and `Cat` can inherit these behaviors. This reduces duplication and makes the code more maintainable.

Example 4: Using Enums to Avoid Repeated Strings or Constants

If you have several repeated strings in your code, consider using an `enum` instead.

```java
public class Order {
  public void processOrder(String status) {
    if (status.equals("NEW")) {
        // process new order
    } else if (status.equals("PROCESSING")) {
        // process processing order
    } else if (status.equals("COMPLETED")) {
        // process completed order
    }
  }
}
```

Here, the order statuses ("NEW", "PROCESSING", "COMPLETED") are repeated as string literals. This is not only error-prone but also makes it harder to change or extend statuses.

Refactored Code Using Enums:

```
public class Order {
  public enum Status {
    NEW, PROCESSING, COMPLETED
  }

  public void processOrder(Status status) {
    switch (status) {
      case NEW:
        // process new order
        break;
      case PROCESSING:
        // process processing order
        break;
      case COMPLETED:
        // process completed order
        break;
    }
  }
}
```

Using Status as an enum ensures that order statuses are centralized. If you need to add or modify a status, you only need to update the enum, and the compiler will help enforce correct usage across the code.

Key Takeaways for DRY

- Applying DRY in Java encourages you to write cleaner, more modular code that's easier to maintain.
- Following this principle can help prevent bugs and improve the overall organization of your codebase.

From the beginning of any project, you should consider this habit; years later, the effort of refactoring will not be too complex to achieve it.

Keep It Simple, Stupid (KISS)

The KISS principle suggests that developers should strive for simplicity and avoid unnecessary complexity. This makes code easier to understand, maintain, and debug.

The principle focuses on the idea that your software product should be easily understandable to use appropriately. Programmers should avoid introducing unnecessary complexity into the code that leads to more errors, is harder to maintain, and is often harder for other developers to understand.

Here are some ideas to achieve the KISS principle.

- If your software product dont need to introduce complicated OOP concepts such as inheritance and polymorphism, don't do it.
- Java programming introduces Generics to make the code more flexible, but at the same time, it makes the code more complex to understand. If your project never takes advantage of that flexibility, don't do it.
- Use simple algorithms solutions instead of complicated algorithms. Along the project, you will have time to refactor and improve it. For more experimented programmers, the most efficient algorithms will be the first choice, but in the end, both approaches will achieve the same goal.
- Single responsibility principle and clean code practices make your code easy to understand and maintainable for a programmer who is not the one who wrote it.
- Avoid introducing external dependencies in your code only because you found an excellent method you can reuse in your project. Methods from external dependencies can introduce potential points of failure. If you can implement it directly in your code, do it.

A simple solution is better than a complex one because simple solutions are easier to adopt and maintain over time.

Example 1: Simple Method vs. Overly Complex Method

Without KISS Principle

Here's a method that checks if a number is even, but it does so in a very roundabout way:

```
public boolean isEven(int number) {
  if (number % 2 == 0) {
      if (number != 0) {
          return true;
      } else {
          return false;
      }
  } else {
      return false;
  }
}
```

This code is unnecessarily complex. It has extra conditions and branches that are not needed.

With KISS Principle

A simple, clear version of the same logic could look like this:

```
public boolean isEven(int number) {
  return number % 2 == 0;
}
```

Example 2: Avoiding Unnecessary Abstraction

Without KISS Principle

Let's say we want to create a class that stores user information. We could create an entire hierarchy of classes, even though we may not need this level of complexity:

```
abstract class Person {
  abstract String getName();
}

class User extends Person {
  private String name;

  public User(String name) {
    this.name = name;
  }

  @Override
  public String getName() {
    return name;
  }
}
```

This example involves creating an abstract base class (Person) and a subclass (User), even though it's not necessary here. If there's no need for a hierarchy (e.g., if User is the only type we need), the base class adds unnecessary complexity.

With KISS Principle

A simpler approach would be to use a single User class:

```
public class User {
```

```
  private String name;

  public User(String name) {
    this.name = name;
  }

  public String getName() {
    return name;
  }
}
```

This design is simpler and easier to understand. We avoid unnecessary abstraction, which keeps the code lean and focused on the immediate requirements.

Example 3: Simplifying Conditionals

Without KISS Principle

Sometimes developers add complex conditionals or logic that isn't necessary. For instance:

```
public String getUserStatus(int userScore) {
  if (userScore > 100) {
     return "High";
  } else if (userScore > 50 && userScore <= 100) {
     return "Medium";
  } else if (userScore >= 0 && userScore <= 50) {
     return "Low";
  } else {
     return "Invalid";
  }
}
```

The above code is unnecessarily complex. The conditions could be simplified.

With KISS Principle

By simplifying the conditions, we can improve readability:

```
public String getUserStatus(int userScore) {
  if (userScore > 100) {
     return "High";
  } else if (userScore > 50) {
     return "Medium";
  } else if (userScore >= 0) {
     return "Low";
```

```
    } else {
        return "Invalid";
    }
}
```

This version is easier to read because each condition logically flows from the previous one. We removed redundant checks, making the logic clearer and more straightforward.

Example 4: Avoiding Complex Loops

Without KISS Principle

Suppose we want to find a specific item in a list of names. A complex solution might use multiple nested loops and conditions:

```
public boolean containsName(List<String> names, String targetName) {
    for (int i = 0; i < names.size(); i++) {
        String name = names.get(i);
        if (name.equals(targetName)) {
            return true;
        }
        for (int j = i + 1; j < names.size(); j++) {
            if (names.get(j).equals(targetName)) {
                return true;
            }
        }
    }
    return false;
}
```

This code has unnecessary nested loops and redundant checks, making it harder to understand.

With KISS Principle

A single loop with a simple condition check can achieve the same result:

```
public boolean containsName(List<String> names, String targetName) {
    for (String name : names) {
        if (name.equals(targetName)) {
            return true;
        }
    }
    return false;
}
```

Or even simpler, by using Java's built-in *contains* method:

```java
public boolean containsName(List<String> names, String targetName) {
  return names.contains(targetName);
}
```

Key Takeaways for KISS

In summarise, the KISS principle in Java encourages writing code that:

- Avoids unnecessary complexity and abstraction.
- Is clear and straightforward.
- Leverages built-in language features when possible.

Following KISS makes code easier to understand and maintain, reducing the likelihood of errors in development and simplifying future modifications.

You Ain't Gonna Need It (YAGNI)

The YAGNI principle encourages developers to avoid writing code that may be needed in the future but is not necessary at present. This reduces complexity and saves time and effort.

This principle also states that new methods that implement new functionality should only be added when necessary. It's a repetitive task in Extreme programming[2] (XP).

Not only do you include cost and unnecessary unit tests, but you create confusion about methods that no one uses in your development team.

Example 1: Avoid Unused Methods or Classes

Problem

Imagine you're developing a library for mathematical operations. While working on the `Addition` class, you think about possibly needing more operations like multiplication or trigonometric functions in the future. Following YAGNI, instead of prematurely creating classes for these operations, you should stick to only what is required at the moment.

---

[2] https://en.wikipedia.org/wiki/Extreme_programming

Code Example

```
// Start with only what is necessary for your current task.
public class Addition {
  public int add(int a, int b) {
    return a + b;
  }
}

// Avoid this unless it's currently needed:
public class Multiplication {
  public int multiply(int a, int b) {
    return a * b;
  }
}

public class Trigonometry {
  public double sin(double angle) {
    return Math.sin(angle);
  }
  // Other trigonometric functions...
}
```

Following YAGNI, you should avoid creating Multiplication and Trigonometry until they are explicitly required by the application.

Example 2: Avoid Overly Generic Code

Problem

In an effort to make code reusable, developers might create overly generic classes or methods that handle all sorts of cases—most of which are not immediately needed. YAGNI encourages focusing on a specific, concrete implementation first.

Code Example

```
// Avoid overly generic implementations
// unless the requirements clearly need it.
public class DataProcessor<T> {
  public void process(T data) {
    // Overly generic processing that might not be needed.
  }
}

// Instead, create only what is required.
public class StringProcessor {
  public void process(String data) {
```

```
      System.out.println("Processing string: " + data);
   }
}
```

Using DataProcessor<T> might be unnecessary if the current requirement is only to process strings. Instead, create StringProcessor and introduce generics only if additional types are needed later.

Example 3: Avoid Premature Optimization

Problem

A developer might add caching, multi-threading, or complex algorithms to optimize a part of the code that isn't proven to be a performance bottleneck. Following YAGNI, it's best to start simple and optimize later if performance actually becomes an issue.

Code Example

```
public class DataFetcher {
   // Start with a simple approach.
   public String fetchData() {
      // Simulate fetching data
      return "Fetched Data";
   }
}

// Avoid premature optimizations:
public class OptimizedDataFetcher {
   private Map<String, String> cache = new HashMap<>();

   public String fetchData(String key) {
      if (cache.containsKey(key)) {
         return cache.get(key);
         // Using cache unnecessarily
         // if the performance gain isn't required.
      }
      // Simulate data fetching
      String data = "Fetched Data for " + key;
      cache.put(key, data);
      return data;
   }
}
```

Use DataFetcher as the simplest implementation and only optimize by adding caching or threading if the need arises later.

Example 4: Avoid Creating Unnecessary Interfaces

Problem

Creating interfaces for every class can lead to excessive boilerplate without clear benefits, especially if there's no immediate need for polymorphism. YAGNI suggests creating interfaces only when you have a use case that benefits from them.

Code Example

```
// Only create the implementation class
// if an interface isn't necessary yet.
public class OrderService {
  public void processOrder(int orderId) {
    System.out.println("Processing order: " + orderId);
  }
}

// Avoid this unless you have multiple implementations:
public interface OrderServiceInterface {
  void processOrder(int orderId);
}

public class OrderServiceImpl implements OrderServiceInterface {
  public void processOrder(int orderId) {
    System.out.println("Processing order: " + orderId);
  }
}
```

Starting with OrderService is simpler and more readable. If you later need a second implementation, you can extract the interface then.

Example 5: Avoid Placeholder Code for Hypothetical Features

Problem

When writing code, you might think of adding placeholders for potential future features. YAGNI discourages adding placeholder code because it clutters the codebase with unused or untested code.

Code Example

```
public class ReportGenerator {
  public String generateBasicReport() {
    return "Basic Report";
  }
```

```java
// Avoid this placeholder unless it's immediately needed:
public String generateDetailedReport() {
  // Placeholder for a future feature
  return "Detailed Report - Not Implemented";
}
}
```

Avoid adding generateDetailedReport() until there's a clear need for detailed reports. Placeholder methods can make the codebase confusing and add unnecessary maintenance.

This example makes more sense when you expose a web service that is still not implemented, creating continuous questions from clients about when it will be ready for implementation.

```java
@WebMethod
@WebResult()
public WriteResponse write() throws Exception {

  WriteResponse response = null;

  try {
    response = new WriteResponse();
    response.setProcessInfo("This functionality is not productive");
    // code omitted for brevity

  } catch(Exception e) {
    throw e;
  }

  return response;
}
```

Key Takeaways for YAGNI

- Simplicity: Writing only what is necessary keeps the codebase clean and reduces complexity.
- Readability: The code remains focused and easier for other developers to understand.
- Maintainability: Reducing unused features and boilerplate code makes it easier to maintain and refactor.
- Reduced Risk of Bugs: Every piece of code has the potential to introduce bugs; writing less unnecessary code reduces the potential for errors.

In summarise, YAGNI is a principle that encourages minimalism and pragmatism.

The core idea is to focus on building only what is needed and resist the temptation to build features based on future assumptions. This results in simpler, more maintainable code with fewer dependencies and fewer unused features.

Loose coupling & High cohesion

The degree to which the different modules/classes depend on each other is called coupling. Loose coupling means modules/components are **minimally dependent** on each other. They interact via **well-defined interfaces** rather than knowing each other's internal details.

As a software designer, your goal should be to minimize the amount of coupling, reducing the number of unnecessary dependencies in every class. Loose coupling improves reusability and maintainability.

Cohesion is the degree to which the methods or behaviors inside a module or class do a related job. High cohesion means a module or class has a **single, focused responsibility** and all its internal parts are closely related to that purpose.

A module or class with well-defined related responsibilities is more likely to be reused.

Modularizing your software using low coupling and high cohesion in your classes allows you to update your functional components individually without breaking the whole system.

Modular design

Modular design is a design technique that decomposes a software system into smaller self-contained units called modules. Each module is responsible for a specific part of the system's functionality and can be developed, tested, and maintained independently. These modules work together to form a complete system.

Dependencies between modules cannot be avoided. In Java, a module consists of an *interface* and its *implementation* class.

To minimize the creation of modules and the dependencies between them, we must keep the principles of loose coupling and high cohesion in mind.

Both Together in Modular Design:

Concept	What it encourages	Result in Modular Design
Loose Coupling	Minimal external dependencies	Modules are independent, replaceable
High Cohesion	Focused internal structure	Modules are meaningful and reusable

Think of it like a Lego system:

- Each Lego brick (module) is internally solid (high cohesion)
- Bricks snap together easily but can be swapped (loose coupling)

Example 1: Web Application

Imagine a web application:

- One module handles **user authentication**
- Another manages **database interactions**
- A third one deals with **UI rendering**

Each of these modules can be worked on by different developers or teams and plugged together via clearly defined interfaces (like APIs or method calls).

Benefits:

- Easier collaboration in teams
- Faster development and deployment
- Lower risk of introducing bugs when updating parts of the system
- Supports scalable and agile development practices

Example 2: Payment System

Let's design a payment system with separate modules for:

1. PaymentProcessor
2. Logger
3. MainApp

Module 1: PaymentProcessor

```
public class PaymentProcessor {
```

```
  public boolean processPayment(double amount) {
    // Simulate payment logic
    System.out.println("Processing payment of $" + amount);
    return true;
  }
}
```

Module 2: Logger

```
public class Logger {
  public void log(String message) {
    System.out.println("[LOG] " + message);
  }
}
```

Module 3: MainApp

```
public class MainApp {
  public static void main(String[] args) {
    PaymentProcessor processor = new PaymentProcessor();
    Logger logger = new Logger();

    double amount = 99.99;
    if (processor.processPayment(amount)) {
        logger.log("Payment of $" + amount + " successful.");
    } else {
        logger.log("Payment failed.");
    }
  }
}
```

This example showed how to break a payment system into separate, logical modules that can be developed and maintained independently.

Example 3: Employee Management System

Modules:

1. Employee class (data model)
2. EmployeeService (business logic)
3. App (main module)

Employee.java

```
public class Employee {
  private String name;
  private int id;
```

```java
  public Employee(int id, String name) {
    this.id = id;
    this.name = name;
  }

  public String getDetails() {
    return "ID: " + id + ", Name: " + name;
  }
}
```

EmployeeService.java

```java
import java.util.ArrayList;
import java.util.List;

public class EmployeeService {
  private List<Employee> employees = new ArrayList<>();

  public void addEmployee(Employee emp) {
    employees.add(emp);
  }

  public void listEmployees() {
    for (Employee emp : employees) {
      System.out.println(emp.getDetails());
    }
  }
}
```

App.java

```java
public class App {
  public static void main(String[] args) {
    EmployeeService service = new EmployeeService();
    service.addEmployee(new Employee(1, "Alice"));
    service.addEmployee(new Employee(2, "Bob"));

    service.listEmployees();
  }
}
```

This example illustrate how each class (module) has a **single responsibility**. The EmployeeService module is reusable and can be used in other systems.

Example 4: E-Commerce Order System

Let's create a **simple Order System** in a modular design for an **e-commerce context** using Java. This example will focus on clarity and maintainability.

We'll split the system into 5 modules:

1. **Product** – Represents a product in the catalog
2. **Customer** – Represents the customer placing an order
3. **OrderItem** – Represents a line item in an order
4. **Order** – Represents the full order (contains multiple items)
5. **OrderService** – Contains business logic to create and process orders

Product.java

```java
public class Product {
  private String id;
  private String name;
  private double price;

  public Product(String id, String name, double price) {
    this.id = id;
    this.name = name;
    this.price = price;
  }

  public double getPrice() {
    return price;
  }

  public String getName() {
    return name;
  }

  public String getId() {
    return id;
  }
}
```

Customer.java

```java
public class Customer {
  private String customerId;
  private String name;

  public Customer(String customerId, String name) {
    this.customerId = customerId;
    this.name = name;
  }

  public String getName() {
    return name;
  }

  public String getCustomerId() {
```

```java
    return customerId;
  }
}
```

OrderItem.java

```java
public class OrderItem {
  private Product product;
  private int quantity;

  public OrderItem(Product product, int quantity) {
    this.product = product;
    this.quantity = quantity;
  }

  public double getSubtotal() {
    return product.getPrice() * quantity;
  }

  public String getDescription() {
    return product.getName() + " x" + quantity + " = $" + getSubtotal();
  }
}
```

Order.java

```java
import java.util.ArrayList;
import java.util.List;

public class Order {
  private Customer customer;
  private List<OrderItem> items;

  public Order(Customer customer) {
    this.customer = customer;
    this.items = new ArrayList<>();
  }

  public void addItem(Product product, int quantity) {
    items.add(new OrderItem(product, quantity));
  }

  public double calculateTotal() {
    double total = 0;
    for (OrderItem item : items) {
      total += item.getSubtotal();
    }
    return total;
  }

  public void printReceipt() {
    System.out.println("Order for customer: " + customer.getName());
    for (OrderItem item : items) {
```

```
      System.out.println("- " + item.getDescription());
    }
    System.out.println("Total: $" + calculateTotal());
  }
}
```

OrderService.java

```java
public class OrderService {
  public Order createOrder(Customer customer, Product[] products,
    int[] quantities) {
    Order order = new Order(customer);
    for (int i = 0; i < products.length; i++) {
      order.addItem(products[i], quantities[i]);
    }
    return order;
  }
}
```

Main.java

```java
public class Main {
  public static void main(String[] args) {
    // Sample products
    Product p1 = new Product("P001", "Laptop", 1200.00);
    Product p2 = new Product("P002", "Mouse", 25.00);

    // Sample customer
    Customer customer = new Customer("C001", "Alice Johnson");

    // Creating order
    OrderService orderService = new OrderService();
    Order order = orderService.createOrder(
      customer,
      new Product[]{p1, p2},
      new int[]{1, 2} // quantities
    );

    // Print the receipt
    order.printReceipt();
  }
}
```

Why This Is Modular

- Each class has **a clear single responsibility.**
- You could replace Product, Order, or Customer modules without affecting others.
- It's **testable**, **extendable**, and **maintainable.**

Divide and Conquer

In any problem-solving situation, try to apply the divide and conquer principle, breaking a problem into smaller subproblems. It is easier to handle a small problem than a whole problem.

The idea is that when our software artifacts - components or services - are implemented, our future problems are focused only on a specific subsystem.

Then we figure out the problem in only particular packages, classes, methods, and some external dependencies.

Separation of Concerns

This principle suggests that different concerns, such as user interface, data storage, and business logic, should be separated and handled independently. This makes code more modular, easier to maintain, and less prone to errors.

The concerns are separated using modularization, encapsulation, and arrangement in software layers.

For example, The MVC architecture pattern uses the separation of concerns principle to turn complex application development into a more manageable process.

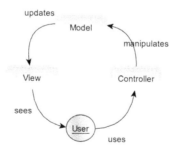

Clean Code

Clean code is a fundamental design principle in software development, focusing on writing code that is easy to read, understand, maintain, and modify, ultimately leading to more robust and reliable software

Clean code can be read and enhanced by a developer other than its original author.

If you want to be a better programmer, you must follow these recommendations.

Clean code has Intention-Revealing names

Names reveal intent. Someone who reads your code must understand the purpose of your variable, function, or class.

Real situation:

```
int sId; //supplier Id
int artDelPrice;
```

It must be refactored to this:

```
int supplierId;
int articleDeliveredPrice;
```

Even with external dependencies:

```
private Z_E2F_RS_Result e2fResult; //ingredients recordset
```

It must be refactored to this:

```
private Z_E2F_RS_Result ingredients;
```

Imagine that we don't have the //*ingredients* comment in the *e2fResult* variable. Then, further in any part of our code, when we try to process this variable, we have the following sentence:

```
e2f = e2fResult[i];
```

And we don't know what e2f means! Well, someone suggests asking the person responsible for this code. But that guy is not at the office. Well, send it an email, and he is on holiday!

But if we adopt names that reveal intent from the beginning, we could avoid these catastrophic scenarios.

```
ingredient = ingredients[i];
```

Clean code tells a story

When we try to fix bugs, when analyzing the sequence of actions (functions, methods), we realize the code does not communicate well the logical flow of these actions. It's a nightmare to decode the meaning of these actions.

This will always happen because our initial design based on the initial requirements changes over time. As developers, we are responsible for refactoring our code to make it a simple story that everybody can understand. For example, look at the following code.

```java
public void performTask(String process) {

  ACMEWebServiceClient.login();
  if (process.equals("core") {
    ACMEWebServiceClient.transfer_buyersCoreData_to_ACME();
  }
  if (process.equals("status")) {
    ACMEWebServiceClient.transfer_buyersStatusChanges_to_ACME();
  }
  if (process.equals("events")) {
    ACMEWebServiceClient.transfer_events_to_ACME();
  }
  ACMEServiceClient.logout();

}
```

Functions should do one thing

Imagine we want to retrieve image objects from an external web service.

We receive image metadata in an array of Strings that informs different values to decide whether an image is valid. One of these values is an image identifier to retrieve the final image object.

```java
private String retrieveImageId(String[] values) {

  if (!values[2].equals("Y") || !values[3].equals("Y"))
    return null;

  String imageId = null;
  //get the first not null value as the imageId
  if (values[4] != null) {
    imageId = values[4]; //imageAIXId
  } else if (values[5] != null) {
```

```
    imageId = values[5]; //imageLIXId
  } else if (values[6] != null) {
    imageId = values[6]; //imageOIXId
  }

  return imageId;
}
```

The previous code is doing more than one thing: validate and retrieve.

Each thing should implement only one abstraction level, meaning only one task. Therefore, we proceed to refactor it.

```
private boolean validateImage(String[] values) {

  if (!values[2].equals("Y") || !values[3].equals("Y"))
    return false;

  return true;
}
```

```
private String retrieveImageId(String[] values) {

  String imageId = null;
  //get the first not null value as the immageId
  if (values[4] != null) {
    imageId = values[4]; //imageAIXId
  } else if (values[5] != null) {
    imageId = values[5]; //imageLIXId
  } else if (values[6] != null) {
    imageId = values[6]; //imageOIXId
  }

  return imageId;
}
```

Here is an example of how to use these new smaller functions.

```
public void syncronizeImages () {

  Response response = api.getImages();
  Row[] rows = response.getRows();
  for (Row row : rows) {
    String[] values = row.getValues();
    if (validateImage(values)) {
      String imageId = retrieveImageId(values);
      //call ULR to retrieve image object
      //code omitted for brevity
    }
  }
}
```

}

Don't comment bad code, rewrite it

Imagine you requested metadata from a list of articles, but the external API, for any reason, includes additional articles in its response object. Before processing their metadata, you want to check that retrieved articles are inside your temporal map of requested articles. Introduces a comment to alert your colleagues.

```
public void syncronizeImages () {

  Response response = api.getImages(mapOfArticles);
  Row[] rows = response.getRows();
  for (Row row : rows) {
    String[] values = row.getValues();
    String articleId = values[1];

    //only requested articles
    if (!mapOfArticles.containsKey(articleId))
      continue;

    //code omitted for brevity
  }
}
```

You can avoid this extra unnecessary comment if you express in your code what you want to communicate by renaming the map variable name.

```
public void syncronizeImages () {

  Response response = api.getImages(mapOfRequestedArticles);
  Row[] rows = response.getRows();
  for (Row row : rows) {
    String[] values = row.getValues();
    String articleId = values[1];

    if (!mapOfRequestedArticles.containsKey(articleId))
      continue;

    //code omitted for brevity
  }
}
```

Comment on what is necessary

You already write good code with readable variables names, small functions, and function names that communicate its goal well. But sometimes it is not enough.

During the analysis and design stage, change requirements happen, and the Software Requirements Specification documents are usually not updated.

For example, export from a SQL database generates a CSV file, which must be retrieved in a java client.

```
public List<Article> loadInitialData(String fileName) throws Exception {
  List<Article> listOfArticles = new ArrayList<>();
  File file = new File(INPUT_FILE_LOCATION + fileName);
  try {
    List<String> allLines = Files.readAllLines(file.toPath());
    for (String line: allLines) {
      String[] fields = line.split(";");
      String id = fields[0].replaceAll("\"", "");
      //code omitted for brevity
    }
  } catch (Exception e) {
    logger.error(e.getMessage());
  }
  return listOfArticles;
}
```

Since this export is manual, it sometimes produces a file with a different encoding format; the java client throws unexpected results.

As this clarification was written in an informal email, it is better to include this information directly in the code for future maintenance.

```
public List<Article> loadInitialData(String fileName) throws Exception {
  List<Article> listOfArticles = new ArrayList<>();
  //once data are exported to csv, edit it and setup utf-8
  File file = new File(INPUT_FILE_LOCATION + fileName);
  try {
      //code omitted for brevity
    }
  } catch (Exception e) {
    logger.error(e.getMessage());
  }
  return listOfArticles;
}
```

Choose simplicity over complexity

As developers, sometimes we use ternary conditional operators that take less space, but when we introduce more variables, the code is not readable or is more difficult to evolve.

For example, when we try to build the article's image URL, we need to evaluate if an image is valid and if the image is not restricted; if it is restricted, we need to assess whether a partner can retrieve this image.

```
String articleImageURL = (imageId <= 0 || (imageIdIsRestricted &&
!partnerCanSeeImage)) ? null : IMAGE_URL + imageId;
```

The previous code can be refactored using nested if-else statements, which is easier to understand.

```
String articleImageURL = null;
if (imageId > 0) {
  if (imageIdIsRestricted) {
    if (partnerCanSeeImage) {
      articleImageURL = IMAGE_URL + imageId;
    }
  } else {
    articleImageURL = IMAGE_URL + imageId;
  }
}
```

Avoid hard coding

Hard coding is embedding data directly into the source code instead of obtaining the data from external sources.

Sometimes we can't avoid including conditional statements using hardcoded values because we need to implement them in a production environment immediately. There are hundreds of reasons why this happens because every company is different.

A company wants to implement in its code validation of customers who have the right to view images from certain providers.

The standard procedure in this company starts with a requirement to the DBA to implement a database function to retrieve a list of providers with this kind of restriction, create param classes for the developers, a period of implementation in a development environment, and its tests in a test environment, and deliver to the production environment.

But the company is facing problems with image author property rights and does not have the resources to implement the requirement, then decides to introduce hard-coded values.

```
boolean picIsRestricted =
  result.getProviderId() == "530636" || result.getProviderId() == "36507";
```

We usually forget the standard procedure to implement the solution because our code is already working. But these hard code values are required in other modules, packages, and classes and may need to validate more providers, etc., and the effort to maintain the code increase exponentially. And I think you know the rest of the history.

You can implement a little function to retrieve external data from a text file.

```
public interface DataService {

  public List<String> getRestrictedProviders() throws Exception;

}
```

Then, you can implement your hard-coded values in an implementation class.

```
public class DataServiceImpl implements DataService {

  @Override
  public List<String> getRestrictedProviders() throws Exception {
    List<String> listOfRestrictedProviders = new ArrayList<>();
    Resource resource = new ClassPathResource("providers.txt");
      try {
        List<String> allLines =
          Files.readAllLines(Paths.get(resource.getURI()));
        for (String provider : allLines) {
          listOfRestrictedProviders.add(provider);
          //TODO retrieve data from a standard database function
        }
      } catch (IOException e) {
        e.printStackTrace();
      }
    return listOfRestrictedProviders;
  }
}
```

Then, you can always reuse the same validation in any place of your code.

```
List<String> listOfRestrictedProviders =
```

```
dataService.getRestrictedProviders();

boolean picIsRestricted =
  listOfRestrictedProviders.contains(result.getProviderId());
```

The day you decide to implement the standard procedure - database function - your effort in refactoring your code will be minimal.

Name your variables according to the context

It is usual to have an attribute that applies to two different objects. For example, an Buyer Object has an email address.

```
public class Buyer {

  private int buyerId;
  private String lastName;
  private String email;

  //code omitted for brevity
}
```

We can see the same attribute in a Supplier Object.

```
public class Supplier {

  private int supplierId;
  private String contact;
  private String email;

  //code omitted for brevity
}
```

When retrieving an email from a supplier object, we may lose the context.

```
String email = supplier.getEmail();
```

Further in our code, we may be unsure if the *email* variable refers to a Supplier or a Buyer.

I prefer to define the schemas of our Objects based on the context.

```
public class Buyer {

  private int buyerId;
  private String buyerLastName;
```

```
   private String buyerEmail;

   //code omitted for brevity
}
```

We do the same for the Supplier object.

```
public class Supplier {

   private int supplierId;
   private String supplierContact;
   private String supplierEmail;

   //code omitted for brevity
}
```

The most advanced editors provide coding assistance features such as variable name suggestions as you type.

```
String supplierEmail = supplier.getSupplierEmail();
String buyerEmail = buyer.getBuyerEmail();
```

Method Overloading

Suppose we already have a function communicating well with an external service.

We send data to subscribe to the external service for a new buyer.

```
public int subscribe(String email, Buyer buyer) {
   //code omitted for brevity
}
```

This function is called from several parts of a program.

```
subscriberId = WSClient.subscribe(email, buyer);
```

Now, we want to send new buyers, but at the same time, we want to inform the external service to take action based on a specific tagged attribute.
If we decide to refactor the function to accept a new argument, we need to change our program in all parts that call the function, even when they dont need to pass the new attribute.

```
subscriberId = WSClient.subscribe(email, buyer, null);
```

We can introduce a new function with the same name but with a new parameter to avoid the unnecessary null value.

```
public int subscribe(String email, Buyer buyer, Integer tagId) {
  //code omitted for brevity
}

public int subscribe(String email, Buyer buyer) {
  //code omitted for brevity
}
```

Only new parts of the program that need to use the new functionality call the new method.

```
subscriberId = WSClient.subscribe(email, buyer, 102911);
```

Method overloading increases the readability and reusability of the program.

Avoid Too Many Arguments In Functions

Sometimes, we write functions containing more than three arguments, like this function:

```
public boolean validateAddress(String street, int number,
  String postalCode, String city, String country) {
  //code omitted for brevity
}
```

As all these arguments belong to an Address concept, we can pass an Object as an argument.

```
public boolean validateAddress(Address address) {
  //code omitted for brevity
}
```

Software Design Principles

Introduction to Object-Oriented Concepts

Object-Oriented Programming (OOP) is a programming paradigm that organizes and structures software design around **objects** rather than functions or logic.

Object-oriented concepts give you a solid foundation for making critical design decisions. I will explain the main concepts and how they are used in designing object-oriented systems and guide you through examples.

Class and Objects

A **class** is a blueprint, template or prototype that describes what an object will be. It defines the structure (attributes or properties) and behavior (methods) of an object. We must design a class before creating an object.

An **object** is an instance of a class with specific data and functionality. When we create an object, we create real-world entities such as cars, bicycles, or dogs with their own attributes and own behaviors.

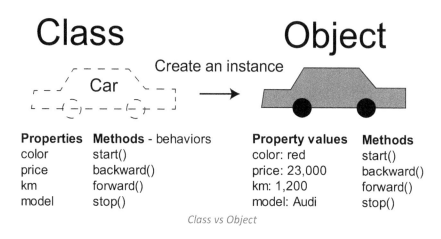

Class		**Object**

Create an instance

Properties	**Methods** - behaviors	**Property values**	**Methods**
color	start()	color: red	start()
price	backward()	price: 23,000	backward()
km	forward()	km: 1,200	forward()
model	stop()	model: Audi	stop()

Class vs Object

The following code shows how this Car template is translated into java.

```java
public class Car {

    private String color;
    private double price;
    private double km;
    private String model;
```

```
    private String brand

    // Constructor
    Car(String brand, String color) {
      this.brand = brand;
      this.color = color;
    }

    // Method
    public void drive() {
      System.out.println("The " + color + " " + brand + " is driving.");
    }

    public void start() {}
    public void backward() {}
    public void forward() {}
    public void stop() {}
}
```

In Java, we instantiate an object via the *new* keyword.

```
public class Main {
  public static void main(String[] args) {
    Car myCar = new Car("Toyota", "red");
    myCar.drive();   // Output: The red Toyota is driving.
  }
}
```

In Object-oriented programming you divide a problem into objects.

Encapsulation and Data Hiding

Encapsulation is the action of bundling data (attributes) and methods (functions) that operate on the data into a single unit (class). In this way, we control access to the data in the object.

Restricting access to specific attributes and methods is called data hiding. Objects should not manipulate the data of other objects.

In Java, encapsulation is possible through *public*, *private*, and *protected* access modifiers. The state of the object is accessed or modified through *public* methods.

Example:

```
public class Car {
  private double km;
```

```
public double getKm() {
  return km;
}

public void setKm(double km) {
  this.km = km;
  }
}
```

When code is spread out and encapsulated, developers know that there is only one way to modify the state of our object: using the *setKm* method. There is no way to manipulate the private *km* attribute directly.

If you want to promote security, your data should not be visible to the outside world

Example:

```
class BankAccount {
  private double balance; // Private attribute

  // Constructor
  BankAccount(double initialBalance) {
    balance = initialBalance;
  }

  // Method to deposit money
  public void deposit(double amount) {
    balance += amount;
  }

  // Getter method to access private balance
  public double getBalance() {
    return balance;
  }
}

public class Main {
  public static void main(String[] args) {
    BankAccount account = new BankAccount(1000);
    account.deposit(500);
    System.out.println("Balance: " + account.getBalance());
    // Output: Balance: 1500.0
  }
}
```

Inheritance

Mechanism where a new class (child) derives properties and behaviors from

45

an existing class (parent).

Inheritance provides the ability to create new classes with new functionalities while maintaining the functionalities inherited. In this way, it promotes code reusability and establishes a hierarchy.

A class with all the attributes and methods that are common to classes that inherit from it is called a *superclass*, a *base* class, or a *parent* class.

A class derived from the superclass is called a *subclass*, an *extended* class, or a *child* class.

Example:

```java
// Parent class
class Animal {
  void speak() {
    System.out.println("Animal speaks");
  }
}

// Child class
class Dog extends Animal {
  @Override
  void speak() {
    System.out.println("Dog barks");
  }
}

public class Main {
  public static void main(String[] args) {
    Dog myDog = new Dog();
    myDog.speak();  // Output: Dog barks
  }
}
```

Example:

In a supermarket context we have the following class.

```java
public class Product {

  private String name;
  private double price;

}
```

Then, the business decides to introduce a Clothing product that manages sizes.

Instead of creating a new class, you derive it from the existing product class because it already contains the minimum required attributes.

In Java, we create inheritance between classes via the *extends* keyword.

```
public class Clothing extends Product {

  private String size;

}
```

This relationship is an *is-a* relationship because when a subclass inherits from a superclass, it can do anything that the superclass can do.

Example:

Let's see how inheritance fits when we recover data from two normalized tables.

A business dealing with food products from different manufacturers defines a Product class.

Product
idProduct
Name
Description
Price
ValidFrom
ValidUntil
CreatedAt
UpdateAt
IdManufacturer

To retrieve product data, we define the following java class.

```
public class Product {

  private int idProduct;
  private String name;
  private String description;
  private double price;
  //code omitted for brevity
}
```

The business shows the product data on a website. Some specific manufacturers want to show its nutrients data.

Using an internal process, the business retrieves this extra information and stores it in a second table.

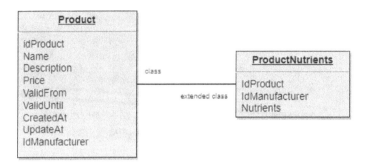

To retrieve the product nutrients, we define the following java class.

```
public class ProductNutrients extends Product {

  private String nutrients;

}
```

When you want to retrieve and manipulate product data and its additional data – nutrients -, define an interface with the following methods.

```
public interface Product {

  List<Product> getListOfProducts();

  List<ProductNutrients> getListOfProductsWithNutrients();

}
```

Polymorphism

- Ability to present the same interface for different underlying data types or classes.
- Achieved through method overriding and interfaces.
Example:

```
// Base class
class Shape {
  void draw() {
    System.out.println("Drawing a Shape");
  }
}

// Derived classes
class Circle extends Shape {
  @Override
  void draw() {
    System.out.println("Drawing a Circle");
  }
}

class Rectangle extends Shape {
  @Override
  void draw() {
    System.out.println("Drawing a Rectangle");
  }
}

public class Main {
  public static void main(String[] args) {
    Shape[] shapes = { new Circle(), new Rectangle() };

    for (Shape shape : shapes) {
      shape.draw();
    }
    // Output:
    // Drawing a Circle
    // Drawing a Rectangle
  }
}
```

Polymorphism means many shapes and is coupled to inheritance.

Polymorphism allows subclasses to define their unique behaviors.

Example:

A Product class defines a *printAttributes* method.

```
public abstract class Product {
  private String name;
  private double price;

  public Product(String name, double price) {
    this.name = name;
    this.price = price;
  }
```

```
  abstract public String printAttributes();

  public String getName() {
    return name;
  }

  public double getPrice() {
    return price;
  }
}
```

But Clothing and Book's subclasses will implement it differently.

```
public class Clothing extends Product {
  private String size;

  public Clothing(String name, double price, String size) {
    super(name, price);
    this.size = size;
  }

  @Override
  public String printAttributes() {
    return "Product{" +
            "name='" + getName() + '\'' +
            ", price=" + getPrice() +
            ", size=" + size +
            '}';
  }
}
```

The Book subclass includes an *author* attribute that is not included in the Clothing subclass.

```
public class Book extends Product {
  private String author;

  public Book(String name, double price, String author) {
    super(name, price);
    this.author = author;
  }

  @Override
  public String printAttributes() {
    return "Product{" +
            "name='" + getName() + '\'' +
            ", price=" + getPrice() +
            ", author=" + author +
            '}';
  }
}
```

The two subclasses override the *printAttributes* method and respond differently when the method is called. Here is a test program.

```
public class TestProducts {
  public static void main(String[] args) {
    Product product1 = new Book("OOP", 9, "MGamio");
    Product product2 = new Clothing("T-shirt", 19, "XL");
    System.out.println(product1.printAttributes());
    System.out.println(product2.printAttributes());
  }
}
```

For every object instance variable, Java calls the appropriate method. Here is the output from the test program.

```
Product{name='OOP', price=9.0, author=MGamio}
Product{name='T-shirt', price=19.0, size=XL}
```

We can create hundreds of subclasses of products, and the polymorphism will allow using all these subclasses precisely like their parent class without any worry about their types.

Abstraction

Abstraction is a process that focuses on the relevant characteristics of a situation, problem or object and ignores all of the non-essential details.

How is this applied in object-oriented software?:

- Hiding complex implementation details and showing only the necessary features of an object.
- Achieved using abstract classes and interfaces.

Example:

```
// Abstract base class
abstract class Vehicle {
  abstract void startEngine();  // Abstract method
}

// Concrete subclass
class Car extends Vehicle {
  @Override
```

```
  void startEngine() {
    System.out.println("Car engine started");
  }
}

public class Main {
  public static void main(String[] args) {
    Vehicle myCar = new Car();
    myCar.startEngine();  // Output: Car engine started
  }
}
```

Abstraction is considered *innate to human beings* because it is a cognitive skill that humans - *programmers* - naturally develop as part of their mental processes.

Here are some examples of abstraction in everyday life:

- When you drive a car, you don't need to know how the engine works in order to operate it. You just need to know how to turn the steering wheel, accelerate, and brake. Do you think, that knowing these minimal functionalities allows you to drive a car? In other words, does it solve your problem?

- When you use a computer, you don't need to know how the operating system works in order to use your applications. You just need to know how to open and close files, and how to use the various features of the applications.

- You can see the essential buttons on your TV remote, and when you press one of these buttons, you don't care what's going on internally on your TV remote. You just want to watch a movie.

This innate ability to abstract information is crucial for software development. Here are a few reasons why abstraction is considered innate to humans:

- Generalization: Humans can generalize knowledge from specific instances to broader concepts. For example, a child who learns what a dog is can generalize that knowledge to recognize other dogs, even if they look different. This ability to generalize involves abstracting common characteristics.

- Concept Formation: Humans have the ability to form abstract concepts that represent categories of objects or ideas. For instance, the concept of "freedom" or "justice" is an abstract idea that encompasses a range of specific situations and contexts.

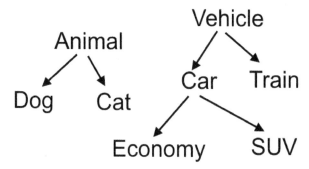

We use abstractions to look for similarities to build categories.

- Problem-Solving: Abstraction is essential for problem-solving. When faced with a complex problem, developers naturally abstract the key elements and focus on relevant details to find a solution.

If abstraction is innate to human beings, why is it so difficult for a software developer to abstract concepts from a business domain?

Abstraction in Object-Oriented Software Development

Abstraction allows an *object* telling to its users what an application does instead of how it does it.

Before becoming developers, we spend a relatively long time learning and developing our cognitive abilities, including abstraction.

We learn to recognize books, cars, streets, and clothes, and they are part of our daily life. And they usually **don't have drastic changes**.

While abstraction is a natural cognitive ability for software developers, abstracting concepts in a business domain can be challenging for several reasons:

- Domain Complexity: Business domains can be quite complex, involving intricate processes, workflows, and interactions between various stakeholders. This complexity can make it difficult for developers to fully grasp the essence of the domain and identify the core concepts that need to be represented in the software.

Software Architecture

We use abstractions to model complex systems

- Lack of Domain Knowledge: Developers often specialize in software development methodologies, programming languages, and design principles, but their knowledge of the specific business domain may be limited. This can hinder their ability to accurately abstract the concepts from the domain and translate them into a software representation.

- Diverse Stakeholder Perspectives: Different stakeholders within a business may have varying perspectives and interpretations of concepts. Aligning these perspectives to create a unified abstraction can be difficult, especially when stakeholders come from different departments, have diverse roles, or use different terminologies. For example, in a B2B Context, developers come from different companies in an API integration project.

- Dynamic Nature of Business: Businesses are dynamic, and their processes, strategies, and objectives can change over time. Adapting to these changes and maintaining accurate abstractions can be challenging, especially if there is a lack of communication and documentation.

- Interconnectedness of Concepts: Concepts in a business domain are often interconnected, and changes to one concept may have ripple effects on others. Understanding these interconnections and abstracting concepts without losing important details can be a complex task.

For example, consider a situation where you have two car and electric bike classes with similar attributes and methods.

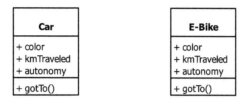

To avoid duplicate code, we need to find a new entity or concept where we can centralize all this information and reuse it in other concepts. In software development, we use abstraction to analyze these common data and move it into a new general concept, for example, a Vehicle.

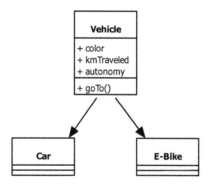

How can we abstract a business concept?

For example, we want to create an Address abstract concept where we can deliver goods. Let's see all possible information that we can include in this concept.

```
company
companyNroEmployees
contact
contactPersonAge
countryCode
city
cityNumberOfDistricts
district
poBox
zip
street
```

```
streetLen
streetIsDangerous
streetHasTrees
email
phone
```

When you create a software model, focus only on things or concepts that include information that is only important and relevant to solving the problem.

We can eliminate information – attributes – that are not relevant to a specific business context.

```
company
companyNroEmployees
contact
contactPersonAge
countryCode
city
cityNumberOfDistricts
district
poBox
zip
street
streetLen
streetIsDangerous
streetHasTrees
email
phone
```

We must conclude with a final Address abstract concept that satisfies our business requirement.

```
company
contact
countryCode
city
district
poBox
zip
street
email
phone
```

Remember, abstraction is a skill that develops over time with consistent effort and practice. By actively engaging with the business domain, refining your critical thinking skills, and utilizing modeling techniques, you can enhance your ability to effectively capture the essence of complex business contexts and translate them into well-structured software solutions.

Exercise

We have identified different concepts in the food business[3]. Try to describe all attributes for every concept that are relevant to the business.

A **buyer** represents an organization aiming to place orders at suppliers to get articles delivered.

A **supplier** represents an organization selling and delivering food articles.

A **customer number** is used to identify a buyer towards a supplier.

An **article** is an item offered by a supplier to buyers.

An **assortment** is a curated list of articles provided by a supplier.

A **buying list** is a list of articles curated by the buyer specifically for one supplier.

An **order** is a request to buy articles to the supplier including payment methods, delivery date, and delivery address. Orders contain of **order positions** that includes specific articles and quantities.

A **platform** is an organization that represents numerous buyers.

An **address** contains a post address and contact information such as an email address.

Behavior

Behavior defines what the object can do and how it acts and reacts regarding its state changes and message passing.

In object-oriented programming, we create behaviors in methods that a class offers to other objects. In practice, we define the behavior of an object through a set of methods.

State

The data stored within an object represents the state of the object. In object-

---

[3] https://app.swaggerhub.com/apis-docs/MGAMIO/selly-order_api/3.0.0

oriented programming, the state of an object is the combination of its original values plus any modifications.

For example, values of the *color* variable in the Car object can be changed from red to green.

We define behaviors to set and retrieve a color change.

```
public void setColor(String color) {
  this.color = color;
}

public String getColor() {
  return color;
}
```

When another object needs this information, it can send a *message* to a car object and ask it what its color is. Messages are the communication mechanism between objects.

```
public class CarAssembler {
  public Car buildCar() {

    Car car = new Car();
    car.setColor("green");

      . . . //code omitted for brevity

    String carColor = car.getColor();

      . . . //code omitted for brevity

  }
}
```

The state of an object is influenced by how the object behaves.

Constructors

A constructor creates space in memory for new objects. In Java and C#, a constructor is a method that uses the same name as the class and has no return type.

You can always use a constructor to initialize the state of an object.

```
public class Car {
```

```
  private double km;

  public Car() {
    km = 0;
  }
}
```

You can use multiple constructors to initialize your attributes for different situations. For example, when you want to sell a second-hand car.

```
public class Car {

  private double km;

  public Car(double km) {
    this.km = km;
  }

}
```

And you, as a seller, initialize the already consumed kms.

```
public class Seller {

  Car usedCar = new Car(1200);

}
```

Interface

The interface defines operations - methods - to describe how users interact with the class through messages.

A method defines a signature that includes the names and types of its parameters, the type of its return value, comments, and exceptions thrown by the method. This way, users fully understand how to call the method and what they can expect from it.

In Java, we create an interface as a set of related methods with empty bodies without code implementation.

Here is when we start to think in abstractions, thinking about all minimal important operations that will help to solve a business problem. For example, the following class shows how it looks like an interface to build a car.

```
public interface Car {
```

```
/**
 * Start the car
 *
 * @throws Exception handle error
 */
 public void start() throws Exception;

/**
 * Get the petrol consumed since a specific date
 *
 * @param sinceDate specify a date
 * @return petrol in liters
 * @throws Exception handle error
 */
 public double getPetrolConsumed(Date sinceDate) throws Exception;

 //code omitted for brevity
}
```

Implementation

Here we implement the methods defined in the interface with complex business logic that users cannot see.

In Java, we use the *implements* keyword to implement all methods defined in an interface.

```
public class AudiCar implements Car {

  //variables that users cannot see.
  private Engine engine;
  private int petrolCapacity;

  @Override
  public void start() {
    System.out.println("Let's start driving");
    //some complex logic
  }

  //code omitted for brevity
}
```

We usually say that interfaces define a contract between the class and the users. By implementing the interface, we deliver the operations we promised to users to solve a business problem.

Overloading & Overriding

If an object contains two methods with the same name but different types of parameters, then we say the method is overloaded. For example, the following class shows two constructor methods.

```
public class Car {

  private double km;

  public Car() {
    km = 0;
  }
  public Car(double km) {
    this.km = km;
  }
}
```

Overloading happens completely at compile-time.

Method overriding happens when a subclass has the same method as the parent class and provides a particular implementation when the method is called.

One way to implement polymorphism is via method overriding, which happens at runtime.

Relationships among Classes

Objects contribute to the behavior of a system by collaborating with one another. An object communicates with another object to use the results of operations provided by that object.

Association

Association is a relationship between two classes that are independent of one another.

Association can be of four types: one-to-one, one-to-many, many-to-one, and many-to-many.

For example, we have the Customer and Address classes.

```
public class Customer {

  private String name;
```

```
  public Customer(String name) {
    this.name = name;
  }

  // getters and setters omitted for brevity
}
```

```
public class Address {

  private String street;

  public Address(String street) {
    this.street = street;
  }

  // getters and setters omitted for brevity
}
```

We associate these two separate classes through their objects in the *main* method.

```
public class TestAssociation {
  public static void main(String[] args) {
    Customer customer = new Customer("Adam Fox");
    Address address = new Address("BornStrasse 12");
    System.out.println(customer.getName + " lives in " +
                       address.getStreet() + " street");
  }
}
```

Output

```
Adam Fox lives in BornStrasse 12 street
```

Aggregation

Aggregation is a particular case of association and is unidirectional.

The aggregated objects have their life cycle, but one of the objects is the owner of the HAS-A relationship.

For example, a *supplier* can provide products in a B2B food business.

```
public class Supplier {
  private String name;
```

```
  public Supplier(String name) {
    this.name = name;
  }

  // getters and setters omitted for brevity
}
```

And a *buyer* can order products from one specific *supplier*.

```
public class Buyer {

  private String name;
  private Supplier supplier;

  public Buyer(String name, Supplier supplier) {
    this.name = name;
    this.supplier = supplier;
  }

  // getters and setters omitted for brevity
}
```

We can see that *buyer* class is the owner of the *has-a* relationship, buyer has-a supplier. We implement this aggregation relationship in the main method.

```
public class TestAggregation {
  public static void main(String[] args) {
    Supplier supplier = new Supplier("ACMEFood");
    Buyer buyer = new Buyer("burguerKing", supplier);
  }
}
```

If the buyer object is destroyed, the supplier object continues its life cycle.

Composition

The composition represents a *part-of* relationship containing an object that cannot exist independently. It is more restrictive than aggregation.

For example, an order is always shipped to a fixed address.

```
public class Address {

  private String street;

  public Address(String street) {
```

```
    this.street = street;
  }

  // getters and setters omitted for brevity
}
```

Since the *address* is part of the *order*, we create it inside the *order* class.

```
public class Order {
  private final int nro;
  private final Address address;

  public Order(int nro) {
    this.nro = nro;
    Address address = new Address("Roshental 12");
    this.address = address;
  }

  // getters and setters omitted for brevity
}
```

Test of composition from the *main* method.

```
public class TestComposition {
  public static void main(String[] args) {
    Order order = new Order(11);
  }
}
```

When the order object is destroyed, the address object is also destroyed.

Create Classes by reusing Objects from other Classes.

The aggregation and composition provide a mechanism for building classes from other classes. In Java, we usually create a class with instance variables that references one or more objects of other classes.

The benefit of separating one class from another one is the Reuse.

For example, in a shopping context, we need a list of requested items and an *Address* class where to deliver an order.

```
public class Order {

  private int clientId;
  private List<Item> orderItems;
```

```
    private Address shippingAddress;

    //code omitted for brevity
}
```

We build an *Item* class including an *Article* class.

```
public class Item {

    private Article article;
    private double quantity;

    //code omitted for brevity
}
```

And the *Article* class includes enough attributes to support the shopping business.

```
public class Article {
    private int id;
    private String name;
    private double deliveryPrice;
    //code omitted for brevity
}
```

Even we can reuse the *Article* class to support a search request.

```
public class SearchResponse {
    private List<Article> articles;
    //code omitted for brevity
}
```

What happens if the business wants to introduce articles in a country where some articles are forbidden to trade?

We cannot add a new attribute called *tradable* to the Article class because we will never use it in normal countries.

Here, we can use the other technique to build new classes: inheritance.

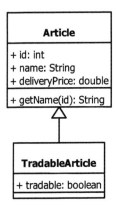

Now, we can support the new requirement for the new country.

```
public class SearchResponse {

  private List<TradableArticle> articles;

  //code omitted for brevity
}
```

We can reuse our classes even out of context. For example, in a Bank context, we need an *Address* class to contact a customer.

```
public class Customer {

  private int customerId;
  private String lastName;
  private Address address;

  //code omitted for brevity
}
```

Advantages of object-oriented programming

Object-oriented programming (OOP) is a programming paradigm that uses objects and classes to structure code. It offers several advantages, which have contributed to its popularity and widespread use in software development:

- Modularity: OOP promotes modularity by encapsulating objects and their behaviors within classes. This allows developers to break down a complex system into smaller, manageable parts, making it easier to understand, maintain, and debug.

- Reusability: OOP encourages code reusability through inheritance and polymorphism. Developers can create new classes by inheriting properties and behaviors from existing classes, reducing redundancy and promoting a "write once, use many times" approach.

- Flexibility and Extensibility: OOP allows for easy modification and extension of existing code. You can add new classes and methods without altering the existing codebase, reducing the risk of introducing bugs in previously working code.

- Abstraction: Abstraction is a key concept in OOP, where you model real-world entities as objects and focus on essential properties and behaviors while hiding unnecessary details. This simplifies problem-solving and enhances code clarity.

- Encapsulation: OOP supports encapsulation by bundling data (attributes) and functions (methods) into objects. Access to an object's internal state is controlled through well-defined interfaces, promoting data integrity and security.

- Organization: OOP provides a natural way to organize code, making it more intuitive for developers to work collaboratively on large projects. Classes and objects mirror the structure of the problem domain, making it easier to map real-world concepts to code.

- Maintainability: OOP code tends to be more maintainable because of its modular and organized nature. Changes and updates can be made to specific classes or objects without affecting the entire system, reducing the risk of introducing unintended side effects.

- Testability: OOP code is often easier to test since objects can be isolated and tested independently, leading to more comprehensive and efficient testing strategies.

- Code Understandability: OOP promotes a closer alignment between code and real-world concepts, making the codebase more understandable to developers, even those who didn't write the original code.

- Support for Large-Scale Development: OOP is well-suited for large-scale software development projects. Its inherent structure and organization facilitate teamwork, reduce development time, and enhance project manageability.

- Community and Ecosystem: OOP has a vast and mature ecosystem of libraries, frameworks, and tools, making it easier to find resources and solutions for common programming tasks.

- Cross-Disciplinary Applications: OOP is applicable to various domains and industries, making it a versatile paradigm suitable for a wide range of software development projects.

While OOP offers numerous advantages, it's important to note that it may not always be the best choice for every project or problem. The choice of programming paradigm should align with the specific requirements, constraints, and goals of the software being developed.

UML Diagrams for developers

The Unified Modeling Language is a graphical notation for modeling systems and conveying user software requirements. All developers must understand this notation before starting programming.

UML is not only pretty pictures. Instead, they communicate the software design decisions to programmers.

Why do we model?

- We build models to understand better the system we are developing.
- Models document the design decisions we have made.
- Models allow an open discussion in the development team before starting programming.
- It speeds up the implementation stage because potential technical issues are discussed during the design stage.
- Explain our software design proposal to external partners.

UML Class Notation

A class is a template for creating objects providing initial values for state (attributes) and behavior (operations). Each attribute has a type. Each operation has a signature.

FlyerComposerService
- qrService: QRService - imageService: ImageService - pdfService: PDFService
+ composerFlyer(qrText: String[*], text: String, image: byte[*], nroFlyers: int): byte[*]

From the figure above:

- The first compartment describes the class name.
- The second compartment describes the attributes with its visibility, private(-) or public(+), and their data types.
- The third compartment describes the operations and their return types.

The following section shows how these compartments are translated into code.

```
public class FlyerComposerService {

  private QRService qrService;
  private ImageService imageService;
  private PDFService pdfService;

  public byte[] composeFlyer(String[] qrText,
    String text,
    byte[] image,
    int nroFlyers) {
    //code omitted for brevity
  }
}
```

Relationships among classes

UML conveys how a class is related to other classes. Let's see the kind of relationships that matter to software design.

Association

An association draws a solid line connecting two classes. It could be named by a verb (using role names) that reflects the business problem domain we are modeling. The following diagram shows two classes that need to communicate with each other.

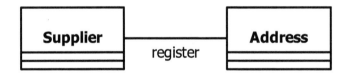

Aggregation

Aggregation is a particular association type representing a *has-a* relationship and is displayed as a solid line with an unfilled diamond at the association end.

A child class object can exist without the parent class object. In the following diagram, if you delete the Buyer class (parent), the Supplier class (child) still exists.

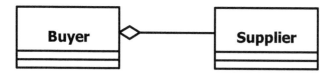

Composition

Composition is a particular type of aggregation where parts are destroyed when the whole is destroyed. The relationship is displayed as a solid line with a filled diamond at the association end.

A child class object cannot exist without the parent class object. In the following diagram, if you delete the Order class (parent), the Address class (child) is also deleted.

Dependency

Dependency is a relationship used to show that some class requires or depends on another class or interface. In other words, some class provides (supplier) particular functionalities that others require (client).

In this case, the *FlyerComposerService* class is the client that requires specific functionality from the *ImageService* class, the supplier.

Inheritance (or Generalization)

A Generalization is a relationship between a more general class and a more specific class. It represents an *is-a* relationship. The specific class inherits the features of the more general class.

Realization

Realization is a relationship where one class realizes or implements the specification defined in another class (usually an interface).

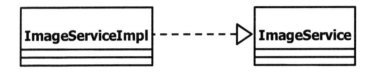

Defining and creating interfaces is an excellent approach to building software to is extendable.

The implemented code reflects the intent of the UML designer.

The following class diagram shows all dependencies a flyer composer service needs to achieve its goals.

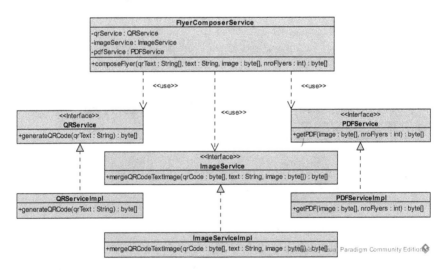

For example, we can see how the *QRService* interface is implemented into code.

```
public interface QRService {
  byte[] generateQRCode(String qrText) throws Exception;
}
```

In addition, we can see how the *QRServiceImpl* class is implemented into code

```
public class QRServiceImpl implements QRService {
  @Override
  public byte[] generateQRCode(String qrText) throws Exception {

  //code omitted for brevity
  }
}
```

Why do we model with UML?

Unified Modeling Language (UML) is a visual language used in software engineering to model, design, and document software systems and their components. There are several reasons why we use UML for modeling:

- **Visualization**: UML provides a graphical representation of a software system, which makes it easier for stakeholders, including developers, designers, and non-technical team members, to understand and discuss the system's structure and behavior. Visual models are often more intuitive and accessible than lines of code or textual descriptions.

- **Communication**: UML acts as a common language for communication between different stakeholders involved in software development, such as developers, architects, project managers, and clients. It bridges the gap between technical and non-technical team members by providing a visual representation that is easy to grasp.

- **Abstraction**: UML allows for the abstraction of complex systems into simpler, high-level models. This abstraction helps in focusing on essential aspects of the system while temporarily ignoring implementation details, promoting clarity and a better understanding of the problem domain.

- **Analysis and Design**: UML is a valuable tool for both the analysis and design phases of software development. During analysis, it helps in understanding user requirements and defining system behavior. During design, it aids in creating a blueprint for the software's architecture and structure.

- Documentation: UML diagrams serve as documentation for software systems. They provide a structured and organized way to capture and communicate design decisions, architectural choices, and system behavior. This documentation is useful for future reference, maintenance, and knowledge transfer.

- Validation: UML models can be used to validate and verify the correctness of a software design before implementation. By simulating and testing models, potential issues and conflicts can be identified and resolved early in the development process, reducing the cost of fixing problems later.

- Code Generation: Some UML modeling tools offer the capability to generate code from UML diagrams, speeding up the development process and ensuring consistency between the design and implementation.

- Reverse Engineering: UML can also be used for reverse engineering, where existing code is transformed into UML diagrams. This is useful for understanding and documenting legacy systems or when working on projects with limited or outdated documentation.

- Collaboration: UML facilitates collaboration among team members by providing a shared visual representation of the system. It encourages discussions, brainstorming, and consensus-building among stakeholders.

- Maintenance: UML models are beneficial for software maintenance. They make it easier to identify areas that need modification, assess the impact of changes, and update documentation accordingly.

In summary, UML is a valuable tool in software engineering because it enhances communication, aids in analysis and design, provides documentation, supports validation, and promotes collaboration among stakeholders. It is a versatile and widely accepted standard for modeling software systems, contributing to the success of software development projects.

SOLID Principles

In the realm of software engineering, few concepts have had as profound an impact on code quality, maintainability, and scalability as the SOLID principles. These five guiding tenets—**S**ingle Responsibility, **O**pen/Closed, **L**iskov Substitution, **I**nterface Segregation, and **D**ependency Inversion—represent a foundational framework upon which modern software design is built. They are the cornerstone of clean, robust, and adaptable code.

SOLID principles tell you how to arrange your functions into classes and how those classes should be interrelated. Robert C. Martin[4] introduced it.

Whether you are a seasoned programmer seeking to reinforce your expertise or a novice developer eager to grasp the essentials of SOLID design, this section provides a comprehensive roadmap to understanding and mastering these fundamental principles.

Let's look at each SOLID principle in detail and then move on to the other principles.

Single Responsibility Principle (SRP)

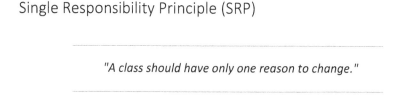

"A class should have only one reason to change."

This principle states that **a class should only have one responsibility**.

Following SRP ensures that a class is easier to understand, test, and maintain. When a class has multiple responsibilities, changes in one responsibility can affect the other, leading to bugs and code that is harder to maintain.

Example 1: File Handling (Violation of SRP)

In this example, a single class handles multiple responsibilities: reading a file, parsing the data, and displaying it.

---

[4] http://www.butunclebob.com/ArticleS.UncleBob.PrinciplesOfOod

```
// Violates SRP
public class FileManager {
  public void readFile(String filePath) {
    System.out.println("Reading file: " + filePath);
    // Code to read the file
  }

  public void parseData() {
    System.out.println("Parsing file data...");
    // Code to parse the file data
  }

  public void displayData() {
    System.out.println("Displaying data...");
    // Code to display the parsed data
  }
}
```

If the logic for reading a file, parsing, or displaying data changes, this single class will need to be modified multiple times, violating SRP.

Refactoring to Follow SRP

Let's split the responsibilities into separate classes.

```
// Class responsible for reading a file
public class FileReader {
  public String readFile(String filePath) {
    System.out.println("Reading file: " + filePath);
    // Simulated file content
    return "file content";
  }
}

// Class responsible for parsing data
public class DataParser {
  public String parseData(String fileContent) {
    System.out.println("Parsing file content...");
    // Simulated parsed data
    return "parsed data";
  }
}

// Class responsible for displaying data
public class DataDisplayer {
  public void displayData(String data) {
    System.out.println("Displaying data: " + data);
  }
}
```

Now, these classes can work together:

76

```
public class Main {
  public static void main(String[] args) {
    FileReader fileReader = new FileReader();
    String content = fileReader.readFile("data.txt");

    DataParser dataParser = new DataParser();
    String parsedData = dataParser.parseData(content);

    DataDisplayer dataDisplayer = new DataDisplayer();
    dataDisplayer.displayData(parsedData);
  }
}
```

Here:

- FileReader is responsible only for reading the file.
- DataParser is responsible only for parsing the content.
- DataDisplayer is responsible only for displaying the data.

Example 2: User Management System (Violation of SRP)

```
public class UserManager {
  public void addUser(String name, String email) {
    System.out.println("Adding user: " + name);
    // Code to add a user
  }

  public void sendEmail(String email, String message) {
    System.out.println("Sending email to: " + email);
    // Code to send email
  }

  public void generateReport() {
    System.out.println("Generating report...");
    // Code to generate user report
  }
}
```

Here, *UserManager* handles:

- User management.
- Email sending.
- Report generation.

Refactored Version to Follow SRP

```
// Class for managing users
```

```
public class UserService {
  public void addUser(String name, String email) {
    System.out.println("Adding user: " + name);
    // Code to add a user
  }
}

// Class for sending emails
public class EmailService {
  public void sendEmail(String email, String message) {
    System.out.println("Sending email to: " + email);
    // Code to send email
  }
}

// Class for generating reports
public class ReportService {
  public void generateReport() {
    System.out.println("Generating report...");
    // Code to generate user report
  }
}
```

Now, the Main class or a controller can use these services together:

```
public class Main {
  public static void main(String[] args) {
    UserService userService = new UserService();
    userService.addUser("John Musk", "john@example.dev");

    EmailService emailService = new EmailService();
    emailService.sendEmail("john@example.dev", "Welcome!");

    ReportService reportService = new ReportService();
    reportService.generateReport();
  }
}
```

Example 3: Payment and Card Teams (Violation of SRP)

For instance, imagine an online store that issues its cards for its customers, and from the beginning, the Payment and Card teams are in mutual agreement to apply for interest and to lock cards from customers who are in late payments for 14 days or more.

In the following Code, we have the first implementation of the Payment Class, which supports both requirements.

```
public class Payment {
  public static final int MAX_DAYS = 14;
```

```
public void batch(List<Customer> customers) {
  for (Customer customer : customers) {
    int nDays = latePaymentDays(customer);
    if (nDays >= MAX_DAYS) {
      applyLatePaymentInterest(customer);
      lockCard(customer);
    }
  }
 }
}
```

The Problem: A Class has more than one responsibility

But suddenly, the Cards team wants to change the validation to 10 days. However, the Payments team manages other policies related to when interests by late payment are applied. As a result, the Payments team disagrees with the Cards team. Moreover, both teams are stuck on how to proceed.

This scenario is a clear example of how this Class design violates the Single Responsibility Principle. The Payment class has more than one reason to change and breaks the Payments team's business logic if they accept the Cards team's requirement.

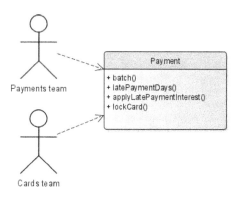

Payment class

The previous figure shows the Payment Class with different responsibilities

The solution: Create Classes with only one responsibility

What do we need to do? In this scenario, we can apply the Single Responsibility Principle.

Refactored Version to Follow SRP

We move the *lockCard()* responsibility to a new Card Class. This technique is most known as refactoring.

```
public class Card {
  public static final int MAX_DAYS = 10;
  public void batch(List customers) {
    for (Customer customer : customers) {
      int nDays = Payment.latePaymentDays(customer);
      if (nDays >= MAX_DAYS) {
        lockCard(customer);
      }
    }
  }
}
```

After that change and following clean code[5] principles, we can see how it looks the new Payment Class (refactored as well).

```
public class Payment {
  public static final int MAX_DAYS = 14;
  public void batch(List<Customer> customers) {
    for (Customer customer : customers) {
      int nDays = latePaymentDays(customer);
      if (nDays >= MAX_DAYS) {
        applyLatePaymentInterest(customer);
      }
    }
  }
}
```

Now, new changes to the MAX_DAYS variable will only depend on the requirements of every team separately. The following figure shows the Classes for different actors, without conflicts.

Therefore, the Payment Class is only responsible for supporting to the Payments team, and the Card Class is solely responsible for supporting the Cards team.

Also, when new features arrive, then we need to distinct in which class to include it. Moreover, this is related to the High Cohesion concept, which help us to group similar functions inside a Class, and that have the same purpose served by that class.

---

[5] https://codersite.dev/clean-code/

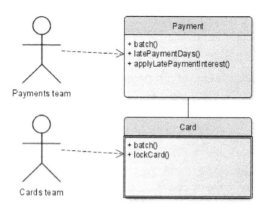

Classes for different actors

Use this principle as a tool when translating business software requirements into technical specifications.

Key Takeaways for SRP

- When you find that a class has many responsibilities, delegate unrelated responsibilities to new classes; in this way, each class will have only one responsibility and one reason to change.

- This principle is intended to separate behaviors into different classes so that if bugs arise due to your change, they don't affect other classes with unrelated behaviors.

- When you implement the single responsibility principle by abstracting your classes via interfaces, your code will be more adaptable to changing requirements in the way Agile frameworks demand.

- The advantages of having a single responsibility are that classes are easier to test, easier to understand their purpose, and easier to maintain.

- Enhanced Collaboration: Developers can work on different responsibilities simultaneously.

In conclusion, once you identify classes that have too many responsibilities, use this refactoring technique to create smaller classes with single responsibilities and focused only on one business actor.

Open-Closed Principle (OCP)

*A class, module, or function should be open for extension
but closed for modification.*

This means you should design your classes and modules so that you can add new functionality without changing the existing code. This reduces the risk of introducing bugs when the software is modified and makes it easier to extend functionality.

Bertrand Meyer[6] coined the principle, suggesting that we should build software to be extendable without touching its current code implementation.

One scenario that violates this principle is when we change one of our classes and realize that we need to adapt all its depending classes.

Steps to Implement OCP in Java

1. **Design using Abstraction**: Use interfaces or abstract classes.
2. **Follow Dependency Inversion Principle**: Depend on abstractions, not concrete implementations.
3. **Use Polymorphism**: Rely on polymorphic behavior for extending functionality.

Example 1: Shape Calculation

Without OCP (Violation)

```
class Rectangle {
  double length;
  double width;

  public Rectangle(double length, double width) {
    this.length = length;
    this.width = width;
  }

  public double calculateArea() {
```

[6] https://en.wikipedia.org/wiki/Object-Oriented_Software_Construction

```
    return length * width;
  }
}

class Circle {
  double radius;

  public Circle(double radius) {
    this.radius = radius;
  }

  public double calculateArea() {
    return Math.PI * radius * radius;
  }
}

class AreaCalculator {
  public double calculateTotalArea(Object[] shapes) {
    double totalArea = 0;
    for (Object shape : shapes) {
        if (shape instanceof Rectangle) {
            Rectangle rectangle = (Rectangle) shape;
            totalArea += rectangle.calculateArea();
        } else if (shape instanceof Circle) {
            Circle circle = (Circle) shape;
            totalArea += circle.calculateArea();
        }
    }
    return totalArea;
  }
}
```

Here, if a new shape like Triangle is added, we must modify the AreaCalculator class, violating OCP.

With OCP

```
// Define a common abstraction
interface Shape {
  double calculateArea();
}

// Concrete implementations
class Rectangle implements Shape {
  private double length;
  private double width;

  public Rectangle(double length, double width) {
    this.length = length;
    this.width = width;
  }

  @Override
  public double calculateArea() {
```

```
    return length * width;
  }
}

class Circle implements Shape {
  private double radius;

  public Circle(double radius) {
    this.radius = radius;
  }

  @Override
  public double calculateArea() {
    return Math.PI * radius * radius;
  }
}

// New Shape: Triangle
class Triangle implements Shape {
  private double base;
  private double height;

  public Triangle(double base, double height) {
    this.base = base;
    this.height = height;
  }

  @Override
  public double calculateArea() {
    return 0.5 * base * height;
  }
}

// Open for extension
class AreaCalculator {
  public double calculateTotalArea(Shape[] shapes) {
    double totalArea = 0;
    for (Shape shape : shapes) {
      totalArea += shape.calculateArea();
    }
    return totalArea;
  }
}
```

Now, adding a new shape like Triangle requires no changes to the AreaCalculator.

Example 2: Notification System
Without OCP (Violation)

```
class NotificationService {
  public void sendNotification(String type, String message) {
    if (type.equals("EMAIL")) {
        System.out.println("Sending Email: " + message);
```

```
    } else if (type.equals("SMS")) {
        System.out.println("Sending SMS: " + message);
    }
  }
}
```

Adding a new notification type (e.g., "Push Notification") would require modifying the NotificationService class.

With OCP

```
// Abstract notifier
interface Notifier {
  void send(String message);
}

// Email notifier
class EmailNotifier implements Notifier {
  @Override
  public void send(String message) {
    System.out.println("Sending Email: " + message);
  }
}

// SMS notifier
class SMSNotifier implements Notifier {
  @Override
  public void send(String message) {
    System.out.println("Sending SMS: " + message);
  }
}

// New notifier: Push notification
class PushNotifier implements Notifier {
  @Override
  public void send(String message) {
    System.out.println("Sending Push Notification: " + message);
  }
}

// Notification service
class NotificationService {
  public void notify(Notifier notifier, String message) {
    notifier.send(message);
  }
}
```

Now, adding a new notification type only requires creating a new Notifier implementation.

Example 3: Rate Limit Algorithm

When we cannot visualize future requirements

For instance, imagine designing and implementing a rate limit algorithm to control the number of requests allowed for every endpoint in a REST API.

The *RateLimit* class implements an interceptor - *HandlerInterceptor* - that allows an application to intercept HTTP requests before they reach the service, so we can either let the request go through or block it and send back the status code 429.

```
public class RateLimit implements HandlerInterceptor {
  private Map<String, Long> apiPlans;

  @Override
  public boolean preHandle(HttpServletRequest request,
    HttpServletResponse response, Object handler)
    throws Exception {
    //getClientId
    apiPlans = getAPIPlans();
    //build Buckets
    //evaluate request per clientId
    //accept(200) or refuse(429) request
  }
}
```

The number of requests allowed during a time interval is specified in plans; for example, plan A allows to consume 100 requests in 1 minute.

The team wants to retrieve the number of requests by plan from a text file.

Without OCP (Violation)

The following *getAPIPlans* method retrieves those parameters.

```
private Map<String, Long> getAPIPlans() throws Exception {
  Map<String, Long> apiPlans = new ConcurrentHashMap<>();
  Resource resource = new ClassPathResource("apiPlans.txt");
  try {
    List<String> allLines =
    Files.readAllLines(Paths.get(resource.getURI()));
    for (String line: allLines) {
      String[] attributes = line.split(":");
      String plan = attributes[0];
      long capacity = Long.valueOf(attributes[1]).longValue();
      apiPlans.put(plan, capacity);
    }
  } catch (IOException e) {
    throw new RuntimeException(e.getMessage());
  }
```

```
    return apiPlans;
}
```

When suddenly, an unexpected scenario arises

The developer leaves the company, and a new one arrives—for example, You.

As developers, we usually receive tasks to do maintenance in projects that do not belong to us; specifically, we never created that code.

Then weeks later, your team decides that API plans parameters must be retrieved from a database. Therefore, you proceed to replace the *getAPIPlans* method; then, *you break the open-closed principle.* Maybe this rate limit algorithm is still deployed in some infrastructures where there is no possible access to databases.

That is the meaning of the principle; you cannot touch the code that is already implemented and working for a long time. Suppose the code is too complex to understand, not well documented, and includes a lot of dependencies. In that case, we have a lot of probabilities to introduce a bug or break some functionalities that we cannot visualize. Unless it is a bug that we have to fix, we should never modify the existing code.

Even if the code is not well designed or does not follow well object-oriented principles, it could not be easy to extend a class to introduce new functionalities.

The team decides to implement the open-closed principle to support future changes for this scenario. But they need to refactor the code by adopting polymorphism and aggregation.

Polymorphism

Polymorphism is part of the core concepts of Object-Oriented Programming and means many forms, allowing an object to behave differently in some instances. For our scenario, polymorphism will enable the *getAPIPlans* method to achieve its goals in different ways: retrieve the parameters from a text file or a database.

Aggregation

Aggregation defines a HAS-A relationship between two classes. Their objects have their life cycle, but one of them is the owner of the HAS-A relationship. *RateLimit* class has-a *DataService* class.

The following diagram shows the goal of our design.

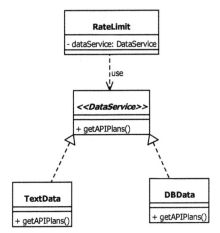

Use of interfaces instead of implementations

Enabling the Open-Closed Principle

Firstly, and thinking abstractly, you should create an interface and define a contract that will include all required functionalities.

```
public interface DataService {

  public Map<String, Long> getAPIPlans() throws Exception;

}
```

Secondly, we move our *getAPIPlans* method to a new *TextData* class that implements the previous interface.

```
public class TextData implements DataService {
  @Override
  public Map<String, Long> getAPIPlans() throws Exception {
    Map<String, Long> apiPlans = new ConcurrentHashMap<>();
    //code omitted

    return apiPlans;
  }
}
```

Thanks to abstractions, we can create a new *DBData* class to implement *getAPIPlans* with different behavior, in this case, to retrieve parameters from a database.

```java
public class DBData implements DataService {
  private DataSource datasource;

  public DBData(DataSource datasource) {
    this.datasource = datasource;
  }

  @Override
  public Map<String, Long> getAPIPlans() throws Exception {
    Map<String, Long> apiPlans = new ConcurrentHashMap<>();
    for (Plan plan : datasource.getAPIPlans()) {
    //code omitted

    }
    return apiPlans;
  }
}
```

Introducing a new abstraction layer with different implementations avoids tight coupling between classes. That means our design is not only coupled to *TextData* class; its design is loose coupling because we can change to *DBData* class and others.

Finally, we refactor our *RateLimit* class *aggregating* an instance of the *DataService* type in its constructor method.

```java
public class RateLimit implements HandlerInterceptor {
  private Map<String, Long> apiPlans;
  private DataService dataService;

  public RateLimit(DataService dataService) {
    this.dataService = dataService;
  }

  @Override
  public boolean preHandle(HttpServletRequest request,
    HttpServletResponse response, Object handler)
    throws Exception {
    //getClientId
    apiPlans = dataService.getAPIPlans();
    //build Buckets
    //evaluate request per clientId
    //accept(200) or refuse(429) request
  }
}
```

If later we decided to retrieve the parameters from a NoSQL database, we would no longer have to touch the code, create a new class that implements *getAPIPlans*, and instantiate this new class in *RateLimit*.

Even if, instead of implementing the *HandlerInterceptor* interface, we implement a *Filter* to design our Rate Limit algorithm, we can reuse the *DataService* interface as one of its dependencies.

Calling to *getAPIPlans* is now fixed (closed for modification). If we want it to behave differently, we implement it in a new class (open for extension) that will follow the contracts defined in our interface.

Our new *DBData* dependency is instantiated in our *RateLimit* class thanks to the magic of the Dependency Injection principle.

Key Takeaways for OCP

- Use **interfaces** or **abstract classes** to define common behaviors.

- Leverage **polymorphism** to achieve dynamic behavior.

- Avoid modifying existing code when introducing new functionality; instead, add new classes or methods that extend the behavior.

These examples demonstrate how adhering to the Open-Closed Principle results in code that is more maintainable and scalable.

Liskov Substitution Principle (LSP)

Types should be able to be replaced by their subtypes without altering the behavior or intended outcome of the program.

For *behavior,* we understand how we abstract an object from the real world and how we describe it in a class or interface.

And for an *intended outcome,* we need to care about what our users or systems expect when they interact with our program composed of classes and interfaces.

Objects of a superclass can be replaceable with objects of its subclasses without altering the application behavior.

In simpler terms, if you have a base class **A** and a subclass **B**, you should be able to use **B** wherever you use **A** without breaking the functionality of your program.

This principle ensures that the subclass does not violate the expectations set by the parent class, such as method behavior, input-output types, or preconditions and postconditions.

Example 1: Violating LSP

Consider the following scenario:

```java
class Rectangle {
  private int width;
  private int height;

  public void setWidth(int width) {
    this.width = width;
  }

  public void setHeight(int height) {
    this.height = height;
  }

  public int getArea() {
    return width * height;
  }
}
class Square extends Rectangle {
  @Override
  public void setWidth(int width) {
    super.setWidth(width);
    super.setHeight(width); // Maintain square property
  }

  @Override
  public void setHeight(int height) {
    super.setWidth(height);
    super.setHeight(height); // Maintain square property
  }
}
```

Here, Square is a subclass of Rectangle, but it violates LSP. Why? Because

Square changes the behavior of Rectangle:

```
Rectangle rect = new Square();
rect.setWidth(5);
rect.setHeight(10);
System.out.println(rect.getArea()); // Expected: 50, Actual: 100
```

The subclass Square breaks the expectations of the parent class Rectangle. This is a violation of LSP because the derived class does not honor the contract established by the base class.

With LSP

To adhere to LSP, you can use better abstraction and avoid forcing an "is-a" relationship:

```
interface Shape {
   int getArea();
}

class Rectangle implements Shape {
   private int width;
   private int height;

   public Rectangle(int width, int height) {
      this.width = width;
      this.height = height;
   }

   public int getWidth() {
      return width;
   }

   public int getHeight() {
      return height;
   }

   @Override
   public int getArea() {
      return width * height;
   }
}

class Square implements Shape {
   private int side;

   public Square(int side) {
      this.side = side;
   }

   public int getSide() {
```

```
    return side;
  }

  @Override
  public int getArea() {
    return side * side;
  }
}
```

Now, Rectangle and Square implement a common Shape interface but are treated as independent shapes. This approach adheres to the LSP because Square no longer inherits from Rectangle and thus doesn't break its behavior.

Example 2: When the Minimal Behavior Required is Broken

Describe an Object with the minimal behavior required

We always expect our base classes to behave in how we define them. For example, in a shopping basket, we expect to add products and calculate all points accumulated by every Product.

Adding products is a natural behavior in a shopping basket, and maybe you think calculating points is optional. But from a business-based point of view, that is what we usually do, modeling objects with minimal behavior **required** based on specific business requirements.

We proceed to describe our *Product* base class.

```
public abstract class Product {
  private String name;
  private double price;

  public Product(String name, double price) {
    this.name = name;
    this.price = price;
  }
  abstract public int calculatePoints();
}
```

The business decides to introduce some clothing products. To behave as a Product, the *Clothing* class inheritances all minimal properties and behaviors from its parent class.

```
public class Clothing extends Product {
  private String size;

  public Clothing(String name, double price) {
```

```
    super(name, price);
  }

  @Override
  public int calculatePoints() {
    //some business logic that calculates the points
    //int points = someBusinessLogic();
    int points = 3; //hardcoded for learning purposes
    return points;
  }
}
```

When we build new classes using inheritance, the new class usually includes new properties or behaviors. We create the *Food* class as well.

```
public class Food extends Product {
  private Date expirationDate;

  public Food(String name, double price) {
    super(name, price);
  }

  @Override
  public int calculatePoints() {
    //int points = otherComplexBusinessLogic();
    int points = 5; //hardcoded for learning purposes
    return points;
  }
}
```

Finally, we create a *Basket* class that executes all minimal functionalities expected from our users.

```
public class Basket {
  private static List<Product> productsList = new ArrayList();

  public static void main(String[] args) {
    Product product1 = new Clothing("Mickey t-shirt", 20.0d);
    addProduct(product1);
    Product product2 = new Food("Bio Sugar", 5.0d);
    addProduct(product2);
    System.out.println("total Points: " + getCollectedPoints());
  }

  public static void addProduct(Product product) {
    productsList.add(product);
  }

  private static int getCollectedPoints() {
    int totalPoints = 0;
    for (Product product : productsList) {
      totalPoints += product.calculatePoints();
```

```
    }
    return totalPoints;
  }
}
```

We use the *Product* base class to call the *calulatePoints* method to get all collected points. In this way, we don't care how every specific class implements the method.

LSP compliance

 interacts with

Program, API, Software

public class Basket {
    addProduct();
    getCollectedPoints();
}

c:\total points: 8

What matters is that every subclass must implement the method defined in its parent class. That is the minimal behavior expected for this business.

Over time, since our program always returns the expected result, we comply with the Liskov substitution principle.

Violating LSP

When the minimal behavior required is broken

Suddenly, the business incorporates a new *Book* product. A new programmer forgot to implement how to calculate points for this new Product, or maybe the business logic of how to do it was not decided yet.

```
public class Book extends Product {
  private String author;

  public Book(String name, double price) {
    super(name, price);
  }

  @Override
  public int calculatePoints() {
```

```
        throw new RuntimeException("Don't support points");
    }
}
```

Therefore, the previous code implementation breaks the Liskov Substitution Principle.

With LSP

One solution could be to create *ProductWithPoints* and *ProductWithoutPoints* classes to avoid breaking the LSP principle, and every new subclass will follow these new specifications.

When you use subtyping, think that there will be a strong behavioral relationship. The minimal behavior required is the fundamental idea of this principle. It is a semantic-based principle.

For example, we expect all cars to be driven on a track; even if the Batmobile subclass can fly or dive into the water, it must include this minimal behavior.

Key Takeaways for LSP

- **Behavioral Consistency:** Subclasses should honor the behavioral contracts of the superclass.
- **Preconditions and Postconditions:** A subclass should not strengthen preconditions or weaken postconditions of the superclass.

- **Avoid Overriding with Contradictions:** Ensure overriding methods do not alter expected outcomes of the superclass.

96

By following LSP, your code becomes more predictable, robust, and easier to maintain.

Interface Segregation Principle (ISP)

Clients should not be forced to depend upon interfaces that they do not use.

In other words, an interface should have only the methods that are relevant to the specific implementing class.

Robert C. Martin defined this principle as *"Many client-specific interfaces are better than one general-purpose interface."*

The idea is to keep interfaces small and focused, avoiding the design of large, unwieldy interfaces that serve multiple purposes. This reduces the risk of changes to an interface affecting classes that do not depend on the changed functionality.

The Interface Segregation principle breaks when clients depend on interfaces that include methods they don't use.

In statically typed languages such as Java, for example, when a change happens in those methods, the implementation class recompiles, and our client should be deployed again even when it doesn't use those methods.

This principle aims to segregate extensive interfaces into different smaller interfaces.

Key Ideas of ISP:

- Create smaller, more specific interfaces rather than one large, general-purpose interface.
- Each class implements only the interfaces it needs.
- Reduces dependency on methods that are irrelevant to a class.

Example 1: Implementing irrelevant methods

Violating ISP:

```java
// Large Interface
public interface Worker {
  void work();
  void eat();
  void sleep();
}

// A robot implements the Worker interface
class Robot implements Worker {
  @Override
  public void work() {
    System.out.println("Robot is working...");
  }

  @Override
  public void eat() {
    // Robots don't eat
    throw new UnsupportedOperationException("Robots don't eat.");
  }

  @Override
  public void sleep() {
    // This warning is confusing for clients
    throw new RuntimeException("method no implemented");
  }
}

// HumanWorker implements all methods correctly
class HumanWorker implements Worker {
  @Override
  public void work() {
    System.out.println("Human is working...");
  }

  @Override
  public void eat() {
    System.out.println("Human is eating...");
  }

  @Override
  public void sleep() {
    System.out.println("Human is sleeping...");
  }
}
```

In this example:

Problem: The Robot class is forced to implement eat() and sleep() methods, even though they are irrelevant to it.

Refactoring to Follow ISP:

Split the Worker interface into smaller, more focused interfaces:

```java
// Segregated interfaces
public interface Workable {
  void work();
}

public interface Eatable {
  void eat();
}

public interface Sleepable {
  void sleep();
}

// Robot only implements Workable
class Robot implements Workable {
  @Override
  public void work() {
    System.out.println("Robot is working...");
  }
}

// HumanWorker implements all relevant interfaces
class HumanWorker implements Workable, Eatable, Sleepable {
  @Override
  public void work() {
    System.out.println("Human is working...");
  }

  @Override
  public void eat() {
    System.out.println("Human is eating...");
  }

  @Override
  public void sleep() {
    System.out.println("Human is sleeping...");
  }
}
```

Now:

- Each class implements only the methods it needs.
- Robot doesn't need to worry about irrelevant methods.
- HumanWorker can still implement the behavior fully.

Example 2: When a Class includes no-related functionalities

There are different reasons why we sometimes find classes with unrelated functionalities. We, as software engineers, must understand its architecture to proceed with maintenance tasks because they still perform the functions the business requires.

Violating ISP:

The following figure shows how a company builds its different internal applications to support its core business based on its legacy systems.

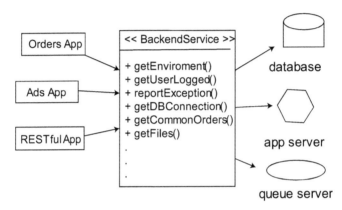

One of these legacy systems is its *BackendService* class. You can realize that includes different no-related functionalities.

If the Orders app needs a change in the *getCommonOrders* method, then all apps must be recompiled and redeployed.

Enabling the Interface Segregation Principle

The business wants to interact with an external partner through an API to retrieve images and store them on its internal application server.

An average developer could reuse the *BackendService* and add new methods to support this integration project.

But the new project does not need to know the environment, retrieve common orders, or even report an Exception that later is sent to a queue manager.

The new application requires only a DB connection, retrieve articles, storing images on an application server, and handling API errors.

Every time you have the opportunity to involve in a new project, use this principle as a tool to analyze your requirements and improve your software architecture.

Think about which methods you can reuse, think about new abstractions, then refactor and move it into a new interface.

Refactoring to Follow ISP:

The following diagram could be a new re-design in your software architecture.

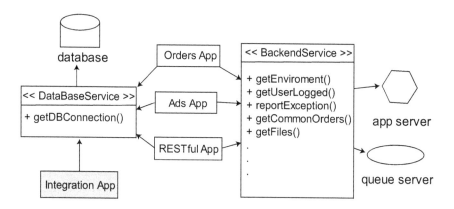

We have segregated a large interface into two interfaces: *BackendService* and *DataBaseService*. The advantage to doing this is that the other apps are not broken, and the new Integration app will use only the method it needs from the new *DataBaseService* Interface.

Once you have the DB connection, develop new, more cohesive interfaces with specific functionalities to achieve the integration app goals.

The following figure shows its class diagram.

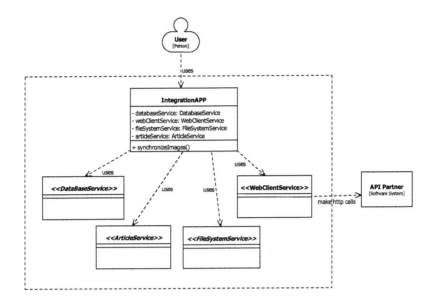

We can see that classes implementing these interfaces do not have to deal with properties and methods that are not of interest to the new integration app.

As software evolves, its common to see *@Dreprectated* annotations, sometimes because companies are constantly refactoring their APIs, resulting in better client requirements support.

Key Takeaways for ISP

- Improved maintainability: Smaller interfaces are easier to understand and modify.
- Greater flexibility: Classes are not forced to implement irrelevant methods.
- Reduced side effects: Changes to one interface do not impact unrelated classes.

This principle helps create more robust and maintainable systems by ensuring interfaces are appropriately designed for the specific needs of each implementing class.

We cannot predict the future requirements, but at least every time you have the opportunity to involve in a new project, try to think about this principle. By doing that, the software could support better future maintenance, refactoring, and reuse.

Dependency Inversion Principle (DIP)

Depend upon Abstractions. Do not depend upon concretions.

Dependency Injection is a design pattern in software development that implements the **Inversion of Control (IoC)** principle. It allows you to write loosely coupled code by injecting dependencies (objects that a class requires to perform its operations) into a class from the outside, rather than the class creating them itself.

To build the most flexible software, we should care that our code dependencies should refer only to abstractions, not implementations. To achieve that, you must introduce an abstraction that decouples the high-level and low-level modules.

Abstractions should not depend on implementation details. Implementation details should depend on abstractions.

Implementation classes change significantly, and abstract things like interfaces change less frequently.

Software designers should take care that every dependency target an interface or an abstract class. No dependency should target an implementation class.

Why Use Dependency Injection?

- Loosely Coupled Code: Easier to maintain and test.
- Improves Testability: Makes it simple to mock dependencies for unit testing.
- Promotes Reusability: Decoupled components are more reusable.
- Simplifies Scalability: Easier to extend the functionality of an application.

Dependency Injection Types

- **Constructor Injection:** Dependencies are provided through a class constructor.

- Setter Injection: Dependencies are provided via setter methods.

- Field Injection: Dependencies are injected directly into fields using reflection (common in frameworks like Spring).

But in reality, we build software as a combination of abstract and concrete classes. That is the case with the *main* Java method, where we initially need to instantiate our implementation classes. Or external concrete dependencies that we trust. To create these volatile concrete objects, we can use Abstract Factory to manage these external dependencies.

Example 1: Constructor Injection

```
// Dependency
class Service {
  public void perform() {
    System.out.println("Service is performing its task.");
  }
}

// Dependent Class
class Client {
  private Service service;

  // Dependency is injected through the constructor
  public Client(Service service) {
    this.service = service;
  }

  public void doWork() {
    service.perform();
  }
}

public class Main {
  public static void main(String[] args) {
    Service service = new Service(); // Create the dependency
    Client client = new Client(service); // Inject the dependency
    client.doWork(); // Use the client
  }
}
```

Example 2: Setter Injection

```
// Dependency
class Service {
  public void perform() {
```

```
      System.out.println("Service is performing its task.");
  }
}

// Dependent Class
class Client {
  private Service service;

  // Dependency is injected via a setter
  public void setService(Service service) {
    this.service = service;
  }

  public void doWork() {
    service.perform();
  }
}

public class Main {
  public static void main(String[] args) {
    Service service = new Service(); // Create the dependency
    Client client = new Client();    // Create the client
    client.setService(service);      // Inject the dependency
    client.doWork();                 // Use the client
  }
}
```

Example 3: Field Injection (Using Spring Framework)

```
import org.springframework.beans.factory.annotation.Autowired;
import org.springframework.stereotype.Component;

// Dependency
@Component
class Service {
  public void perform() {
    System.out.println("Service is performing its task.");
  }
}

// Dependent Class
@Component
class Client {
  @Autowired // Field Injection
  private Service service;

  public void doWork() {
    service.perform();
  }
}

import org.springframework.context.ApplicationContext;
import org...context.annotation.AnnotationConfigApplicationContext;
import org.springframework.context.annotation.ComponentScan;
import org.springframework.context.annotation.Configuration;
```

```
@Configuration
@ComponentScan(basePackages = "com.example")
public class AppConfig {
  public static void main(String[] args) {
    ApplicationContext context = new
    AnnotationConfigApplicationContext(AppConfig.class);
    // Spring injects the dependency
    Client client = context.getBean(Client.class);
    client.doWork();
  }
}
```

Example 4: Sales Report Module

Consider a scenario where you are designing a module to build sales reports.
You fetch data from a relational database, apply complex business logic, and
export it into HTML format by default.

Your design could result in the following class diagram.

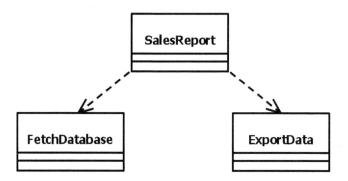

- **FetchDatabase** class fetches sales data from a database.
- **ExportData** class export sales data into HTML
- **SalesReport** class takes data from *FetchDatabase* class, processes it, and
  passes it to *ExportData* class.

You can realize that *SalesReport* class is a high-level module, and *FetchDatabase*
and *ExportData* classes are low-level modules.

The following code shows how *FetchDatabase* class retrieves sales data from a
database.

```
public class FetchDatabase {
```

```
  public SalesData getData() {
    SalesData salesData = new SalesData();
    //after call database, fills salesData object
    return salesData;
  }
}
```

The *ExportData* class will take the *salesData* object and export it into HTML file format.

```
public class ExportData {
  public File exportToHtml(SalesData salesData) {
    File htmlOutput = null;
    //logic to transform salesData into HTML file
    return htmlOutput;
  }
}
```

The Code from *SalesReport* class takes the data from the *FetchDatabase* class and sends it to the *ExportData* class.

```
public class SalesReport {
  private ExportData exportData = new ExportData();
  private FetchDatabase fetchDatabase = new FetchDatabase();

  public void generateSalesReport() {
    SalesData salesData = fetchDatabase.getData();
    exportData.exportToHtml(salesData);
  }
}
```

Good design, but could it support future changes without breaking the system?

Months later, you should also export your sales data in PDF format. Even, you could need to retrieve your sales data from a NoSQL database.

To achieve the PDF format, you will create new classes or new methods. Let's see the second option.

```
public class ExportData {
  public File exportToHtml(SalesData salesData) {
    File htmlOutput = null;
    //logic to transform salesData into HTML file
    return htmlOutput;
  }
  public File exportToPDF(SalesData salesData) {
    File pdfOutput = null;
```

```
    //logic to transform salesData into PDF file
    return pdfOutput;
  }
}
```

We introduce an input parameter to tell *SalesReport* class which output to generate

```
public class SalesReport {
  private ExportData exportData = new ExportData();
  private FetchDatabase fetchDatabase = new FetchDatabase();

  public void generateSalesReport(int reportType) {
    SalesData salesData = fetchDatabase.getData();
    if (reportType == 1) {
      exportData.exportToHtml(salesData);
    } else if (reportType == 2) {
      exportData.exportToPDF(salesData);
    }
  }
}
```

Good job! But wait a moment, what happens if you require to export in XML, JSON, or Excel format?

When you add new methods on the *ExportData* class to support new formats, you must also update the *SalesReport* class. In this way, you are creating a **strong dependency** between the *SalesReport* class and the *ExportData* concrete implementation class.

Changes made to dependent code are always risky.

We say that they are closely coupled and also break the Open-Closed Principle.

Dependency Inversion removes tight dependency between classes

Inversion of Control (IoC), or Dependency Injection allows us to implement the Dependency Inversion Principle.

IoC is a process where an object delegates the definition of its dependencies to another external entity or framework.

The flow control of its main program - *SalesReport* class -, is transferred to some other class or container. That means that the task of creating and maintaining the dependency objects is inverted.

To break the tight dependency between high-level and low-level modules:

- The high-level module defines an abstraction - an interface - and all low-level modules must implement it.
- The creation of dependencies from your main program is transferred to another program or framework.

Your high-level module - *SalesReport* class - now decide which low-level modules can interact with it.

The following diagram shows how the dependencies have been inverted.

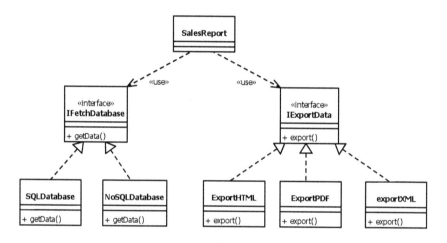

The *SalesReport* top-level module - - now interacts with the standard interfaces. When adding new export data modules, you no longer need to add if else statements in the *SalesReport* class.

Dependency injection is a way to think about and design loosely coupled code, more than a specific technology. Its purpose is to create maintainable software within object-oriented programming.

Let's see how to refactor the code. First, we need to create the interfaces.

```
public interface IFetchDatabase {
  SalesData getData();
}


public interface IExportData {
  File export(SalesData salesData);
```

```
}
```

Next, all low-level modules should implement these interfaces.

```
public class SQLDatabase implements IFetchDatabase {
  @Override
  public SalesData getData() {
    SalesData salesDataFromSQLDatabase = new SalesData();
    //after call database, fills salesDataFromSQLDatabase object
    return salesDataFromSQLDatabase;
  }
}
```

```
public class NoSQLDatabase implements IFetchDatabase {
  @Override
  public SalesData getData() {
    SalesData salesDataFromNoSQLDatabase = new SalesData();
    //after call database, fills salesDataFromNoSQLDatabase object
    return salesDataFromNoSQLDatabase;
  }
}
```

```
public class ExportXML implements IExportData {
  @Override
  public File export(SalesData salesData) {
    File xmlOutput = null;
    //logic to transform salesData into XML file
    return xmlOutput;
  }
}
```

```
public class ExportPDF implements IExportData {
  @Override
  public File export(SalesData salesData) {
    File pdfOutput = null;
    //logic to transform salesData into PDF file
    return pdfOutput;
  }
}
```

```
public class ExportHTML implements IExportData {
  @Override
  public File export(SalesData salesData) {
    File htmlOutput = null;
    //logic to transform salesData into HTML file
    return htmlOutput;
  }
}
```

With Dependency injection, we pass the dependent objects into a software component. It is a requirement to rely on abstraction to set the dependencies.

We apply Constructor injection to our main class

```
public class SalesReport {
  private IExportData exportData;
  private IFetchDatabase fetchDatabase;

  SalesReport(IFetchDatabase fetchDatabase, IExportData exportData) {
    this.fetchDatabase = fetchDatabase;
    this.exportData = exportData;
  }
  public void generateSalesReport() {
    SalesData salesData = fetchDatabase.getData();
    exportData.export(salesData);
  }
}
```

When our main program depends on more dependencies, setup manually dependencies could be complicated. At that moment, we need to rely on dependency injection containers.

A container takes care of creating, configuring, and managing objects. Spring includes its IoC container for java.

If we follow Dependency Inversion Principle, we will avoid volatility in our interfaces, and possible future bugs will be more affordable to tackle. Let's see an example.

Example 5: Apache Log4j Vulnerability

In December 2021, Cybersecurity & Infrastructure Security Agency - CISA - reported widespread exploitation of critical remote code execution (RCE) vulnerability (CVE-2021-44228) in Apache's Log4j software library, known as "log4Shell".

Log4j is used in a lot of companies to log security and performance information from their websites and applications.

When Clients target to an interface
Situation before fixing the bug:

Log4j dependencies found in a java controller

```
import org.slf4j.Logger;
import org.slf4j.LoggerFactory;

public class AgenciesApiController implements AgenciesApi {

  private static final Logger logger
  = Logger.getLogger(AgenciesApiController.class);
  //code omitted for brevity
}
```

The following figure shows the dependencies before the change.

```
∨ ◌ spring-boot-starter-logging : 2.1.5.RELEASE [compile]
    ∨ ◌ logback-classic : 1.2.3 [compile]
        ◌ logback-core : 1.2.3 [compile]
        ◌ slf4j-api : 1.7.26 (managed from 1.7.25) (omitted for conflict with 1.7.26) [compile]
    ∨ ◌ log4j-to-slf4j : 2.11.2 [compile]
        ◌ slf4j-api : 1.7.26 (managed from 1.7.25) (omitted for conflict with 1.7.26) [compile]
        ◌ log4j-api : 2.11.2 [compile]
    ∨ ◌ jul-to-slf4j : 1.7.26 [compile]
        ◌ slf4j-api : 1.7.26 (omitted for conflict with 1.7.26) [compile]
```

Slf4j is a Façade, which means we can implement it with any library. To fix the problem, it was only necessary to upgrade the log4j to the recommended version.

```
pom.xml:
```

```
<properties>
  <log4j2.version>2.17.1</log4j2.version>
</properties>
```

Changes to fix bugs in concrete implementations do not always require changes to the interfaces they implement.

Because controllers were targeting abstract interfaces - Logger – maven updated all implementation classes from the vendor, including the code that fixes the bug.

The following figure shows the dependencies after the change.

```
∨ ⬜ spring-boot-starter-web : 2.1.5.RELEASE [compile]
   ∨ ⬜ spring-boot-starter : 2.1.5.RELEASE [compile]
      ⬜ spring-boot : 2.1.5.RELEASE (omitted for conflict with 2.1.5.RELEASE) [compile]
      ⬜ spring-boot-autoconfigure : 2.1.5.RELEASE (omitted for conflict with 2.1.5.RELEASE) [compile]
      ∨ ⬜ spring-boot-starter-logging : 2.1.5.RELEASE [compile]
         ∨ ⬜ logback-classic : 1.2.3 [compile]
            ⬜ logback-core : 1.2.3 [compile]
            ⬜ slf4j-api : 1.7.26 (managed from 1.7.25) (omitted for conflict with 1.7.26) [compile]
         ∨ ⬜ log4j-to-slf4j : 2.17.1 (managed from 2.11.2) [compile]
            ⬜ slf4j-api : 1.7.26 (managed from 1.7.25) (omitted for conflict with 1.7.26) [compile]
            ⬜ log4j-api : 2.17.1 [compile]
         ∨ ⬜ jul-to-slf4j : 1.7.26 [compile]
            ⬜ slf4j-api : 1.7.26 (omitted for conflict with 1.7.26) [compile]
```

As a software designer, try always to add functionality to implementation classes without changing the interfaces.

Key Takeaways for DIP

- Use constructor injection when dependencies are mandatory.
- Use setter injection for optional dependencies or when you need to change them at runtime.
- Use field injection sparingly, primarily in frameworks like Spring, where dependency injection is handled automatically.

By mastering these techniques, you can write flexible, testable, and maintainable Java applications.

In summary, when SOLID principles are applied correctly, your software infrastructure will tolerate changes, be easier to understand and focus on reusable components.

Soft Skills

Soft skills are the personal attributes that enable individuals to interact effectively and harmoniously with others. In software development, having strong soft skills is just as important as technical skills. Here are some examples of soft skills that are valuable in software development:

1. Communication: Good communication skills are essential for effective collaboration between developers, project managers, and other

stakeholders. This includes the ability to communicate technical information clearly and concisely, as well as the ability to listen actively and ask questions.

2. Problem-solving: In software development, problems are inevitable. A developer with strong problem-solving skills can quickly identify issues and develop effective solutions.

3. Teamwork: Successful software development requires a collaborative effort. Team players can work effectively with others, understand their role within a team, and are willing to lend a hand when needed.

4. Adaptability: The ability to adapt to new technologies, processes, and challenges is crucial in software development, where change is a constant.

5. Time management: Meeting deadlines is crucial in software development. Strong time management skills enable developers to prioritize tasks effectively and deliver projects on time.

6. Attention to detail: Paying attention to details can help developers catch errors, bugs, and other issues before they become bigger problems.

7. Creativity: Creativity can help developers find innovative solutions to complex problems, and come up with new and better ways to approach development challenges.

These are just a few examples of soft skills that can be valuable in software development. Having a strong combination of technical and soft skills can help developers excel in their careers and contribute to successful software projects.

Case Studies

How to interpret a functional description

Imagine that you must design and implement an Order API from its documentation. For example:

Resources and their relationships

*A **buyer** represents an organization aiming to place orders at suppliers to get food and ingredients delivered. This organization can be a single kitchen, a central buying department or any other setup depending on your use-case.*

*A **supplier** represents an organization selling and delivering food and ingredients. These organizations range from local, small agriculture family businesses to large international corporations.*

*A **customer number** is used to identify a buyer towards a supplier. A buyer receives a customer number from a supplier after registration. A buyer will have different customer numbers for different suppliers and might have multiple customers numbers for the same supplier, for example to differentiate departments within the buyer's organization. While technically a customer number is optionally it is very common, and most suppliers work with customer numbers.*

Identify the entities and their relationships

The following figure shows the relationships between these entities.

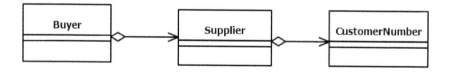

We design different functionalities (in services classes) for every entity that fit the global API requirements, such as creating, updating, and deleting a buyer, and a list of buyers.

We create abstractions about these concepts by creating interfaces.

To retrieve a list of suppliers we already know that we need a buyerId and additional parameters.

Remember to start with classes and methods that are simple and manageable.

```
public interface SuppliersService {
  public List<Supplier> listSuppliers (
    Integer buyerId,
    String supplierNumber,
    String sortBy,
    String sortOrder,
    Integer offset,
    Integer limit) throws Exception;
}
```

To retrieve a list of customers numbers we already know that we need a buyerId, a supplierId and additional parameters.

```
public interface CustomerNumbersService {
  public List<CustomerNumber> listCustomerNumbers(
    Integer buyerId,
    Integer supplierId,
    String customerNumber,
    String sortBy,
    String sortOrder,
    Integer offset,
    Integer limit) throws Exception;
}
```

By *separating concerns* into different specialized classes, reduces the effort of maintenance in future changes because we can localize faster the code where we need to implement, modify, or fix a bug. You will feel confident about changing the code.

Designing a RESTFul API

RESTful refers to implementing REST[7], an architectural style defining guidelines for creating web services.

Business requirement

A company wants to implement an API to allow Restaurants (represented as a buyer) to place orders at suppliers to get food articles delivered.

---

[7] https://codersite.dev/rest-api-overview/

After thoroughly analyzing the requirements, the developer team identified the following *class diagram* showing the main entities and their relationships.

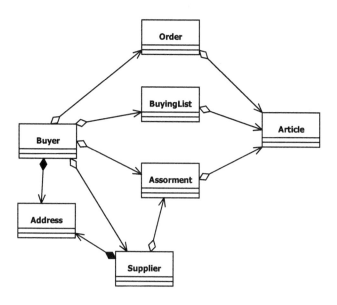

We can see the following *aggregation* relationships and their possible interpretations.

A Buyer *has* Orders
A Buyer can *create* Orders

A Buyer can *create* BuyingLists
A Buyer can *update* BuyingLists

An Order *has* Articles

A Supplier *has* Assortments that *has* Articles

We can see the following *composition* relationships and their possible interpretations.

A Supplier *has* an Address

A Buyer *has* an Addresses

We use API endpoints and HTTP methods to define and implement the specific functional requirements. We should use the nouns representing the entity with the endpoint we're retrieving or manipulating as the pathname.

We use the Buyer entity to design the API endpoints for learning purposes. The following list shows what an authenticated user can do with the API.

GET /buyers
A list of accessible buyers is given

GET /buyers/{buyerId}
Gets the buyer for the requested buyerId

POST /buyers
Creates a new buyer

PUT/buyers/{buyerId}
Updates an existing buyer

DELETE /buyers/{buyerId}
Deletes an existing buyer

GET /buyers/{buyerId}/orders
Gets orders placed by the given buyer

GET /buyers/{buyerId}/buyingLists
Gets buying lists for the given buyer

GET /buyers/{buyerId}/assortments
Gets accessible assortments for the given buyer

GET /buyers/{buyerdId}/suppliers
Gets suppliers accessible by the given buyer

Once we understand software design principles, let's see how they can help us manage the data and create and organize several modules to build the API program.

Identification of Software Design Principles

Design software is an art, and maybe you already built excellent software without using the terminology of software design concepts.

During the last decades, the developer community has identified standard practices to abstract business concepts and catalog them into software design principles.

But when you work for a company with dozens or hundreds of developers, you can use several concepts of software design principles to make your software resilient to future changes. At the same time, it works as a technical communication language between different developer teams.

Separation of concerns

Thanks to this principle, we realize we must divide the API program into distinct parts with unique *responsibilities*.

We need the following artifacts:

- A module, component, *service*, or class responsible for managing all HTTP requests and responses

- A module, component, *service*, or class manages all data from a storage medium.

- A module, component, *service*, or class that forwards the request to the data service, applies some business logic and mappings, and returns a response to the HTTP service

Think about how easy it will be to develop, test, maintain, and change these parts, even for developers who were not involved in the initial stage of analysis and design of the system.

The following diagram shows the necessary layers to achieve the API implementation.

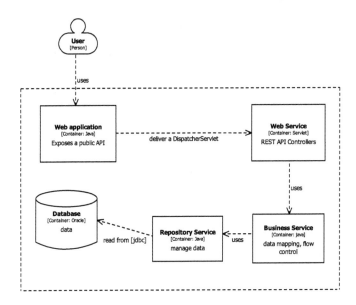

Single Responsibility Principle

To facilitate future changes, we need to create classes with only one reason for change.

For example, if we need to change something related to the Buyer's business entity, we must do it in their class.

```
public interface BuyersApi {

    ResponseEntity<Buyer> addBuyer(Buyer body) throws Exception;

    //enter hier a new method related with Buyer
}
```

If we need to change something related to the Order's business entity, we must do it in their class.

```
public interface OrderApi {

    ResponseEntity<List<Order>> listOrders(int supplierId,
        String sortBy, int offset, int limit) throws Exception;

    //enter hier a new method related with Order
}
```

Interfaces and dependency injection

By using *abstractions*, we create *interfaces* to support the *dependency injection* principle

For example, a *BuyersApiController* class must delegate to a specialized class to manipulate a required functionality once it receives a HTTP request. Then, it **uses** or **depends on** a *BuyersService* class. But at no time does it have contact with a *BuyersRepository* class.

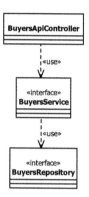

The relation of dependencies happens between interfaces and not in specific implementation classes. In this way, you are decoupling the high-level (BuyersApiController) and low-level (BuyersRepository) classes.

Interfaces and implementations

Interfaces define a contract, abstract methods that communicate what our classes can do. For example, the following class says that creating a new Buyer requires only a Buyer object. In this context, the *BuyersService* class does not need to care about how the *BuyersRepository* class does it.

```
public interface BuyersRepository {

  public Buyer addBuyer(Buyer body) throws Exception;

}
```

The implementation class shows how this *addBuyer* method executes the task of creating a Buyer.

```
public class BuyersRepositoryImpl implements BuyersRepository {
```

```
public Buyer addBuyer(Buyer body) throws Exception {

  String dbURL = "jdbc:oracle:usr:pass/sc@localhost:1521:buyerDB";
  Connection conn = DriverManager.getConnection(dbURL);

  //code omitted for brevety
  }
}
```

Loose coupling & High cohesion

Suppose you migrate your data to a NoSQL database, for example. In that case, you must change the addBuyer method in your implementation class by assigning a new driver value to the *dbURL* variable.

Because we have decoupled the *BuyersService* class and the *BuyersRepository* class through interfaces, introducing changes in the *BuyersRepositoryImpl* class does not break functionalities in other parts of your system.

What matters for the *BuyersService* class is that expect a Buyer object to return.

The same relationship applies between the BuyersService class and the BuyersApiController class.

We create a *BuyersService* interface to help the *BuyersApiController* class manipulate the data from the HTTP requests.

```
public interface BuyersService {

  public Buyer addBuyer(Buyer body) throws Exception;

}
```

The *BuyersServiceImpl* class implements the details with the *help* or the *use* of the *BuyersRepository* class.

```
public class BuyersServiceImpl implements BuyersService {

  private BuyersRepository buyersRepository;

  public BuyersServiceImpl(BuyersRepository buyersRepository) {
    this.buyersRepository = buyersRepository;
  }

  public Buyer addBuyer(Buyer body) throws Exception {
```

```
    //mappings and transformations

    Buyer newBuyer = buyersRepository.addBuyer(body);

    return newBuyer;
  }
}
```

Injecting a class of *BuyersRepository* type in their constructor method, we are assuring our *BuyersServiceImpl* class will be initialized with the required dependencies. Then, we delegate the task of creating a new Buyer to the repository class.

Finally, the *BuyersApiController* class *depends on* the *BuyersService* class.

```
public class BuyersApiController implements BuyersApi {

  private final BuyersService buyersService;

  @Autowired
  public BuyersApiController(BuyersService buyersService) {
    this.buyersService = buyersService;
  }

  public ResponseEntity<Buyer> addBuyer(Buyer body) throws Exception {
    Buyer buyer = buyersService.addBuyer(body);
    return new ResponseEntity<Buyer>(buyer, HttpStatus.CREATED);
  }
}
```

Well, maybe you could manage all these layers in a small company. But when you work in a big company with dozens of developer teams, you most likely specialize in a layer.

For example, legacy systems manage business logic in complex PL/SQL functions. Even some companies create backend customized frameworks to manage all business logic and data; in that case, you don't have contact with the repository layer

Finally, we must create programs (API Servers) that serve data and other programs (API Clients) that consume/manipulate that data, as shown in the following figure.

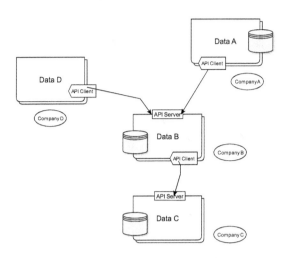

Design a B2B Integration Project

Business-to-business (B2B) is a business conducted between one company and another.

One leading company implements an E-commerce portal to sell t-shirt products from several retail businesses and manufacturers. Uploading of products is done manually by retailers through a user interface.

Identification of a problem

All retailers want to sell their products on the portal because the leading company has a lot of traffic on the internet and is well recognized. But most of the retailers have their websites, so they **duplicate the effort** of the product uploading process.

The business requirement

A retailer sends its product data via a CSV file to the lead company, which uploads it into its database. The lead company then displays this data on its e-commerce portal for selling.

The retailer already has a public RESTful API to retrieve product data from a local database and display it on its own website. So the retailer asks the lead company to use the public API to retrieve thousands of products instead of retrieving this data from a CSV file. And eventually, the lead company can update the product images weekly by calling the API.

Your creative process in action

The company's IT department assigns you the task of **designing** the new software system to achieve the business requirement before sending it to a programming factory.

Well, you already know that software development is a creative process, similar to what an artist does. That means there are different solutions to achieve this automation process.

As a general rule, this is what we usually do when we develop software:

- Analyse carefully the current problem and the business requirements. Ask everything, even what looks obvious.
- Write your proposal on how to build the software. Don't forget your estimate of time.
- Discuss the possible feedback of your proposal and wait for the final approve.
- Start the code implementation.
- Involve all team members during the Test period.
- Refactoring your code to admit changes after the Test period is a good indicator that team members are involved in the project.
- Deliver your software product to a Productive environment.

Know what you are trying to achieve

At this moment, you start to ask and think in high-level abstractions because you are analyzing the requirement, for example:

- The retail business requires an automation process. Do we need a Retail entity?. No, because data from the retail company is irrelevant.
- The retail business facilitates an API server, which means the leading company is the API client that want to consume data. This means exists a data integration process. But which kind of data?. We need data about t-shirt products.
- Both businesses want to exchange data about t-shirt Products, but which attributes?. For example, description, prices, image URL, etc.
- What do we need to do with this data? Move it into a database or a file server?

The company policies influence your design

Your company must corroborate every decision. For example, one policy could be: once you retrieve product data from the API response, save its image object on a file server. There is already a decoupled internal process to create an entry on the database that references the image path and renders it on their website. The decoupling mechanism is essential so that an application process does not interfere with other applications running on the same server and avoids consuming the same physical resources.

Read and understand the requirements documentation

It is usual to read a lot of documentation associated with the project before to elaborate your design proposal. For example:

- The API documentation of the external retailer. Focus on the most relevant sections.
- The Jira ticket where all decisions and changes are documented.
- All communications by e-emails that includes all team members.
- Any external document that clarifies the requirements, such as a flow chart diagram, code examples, limits on API requests, project estimated time, availability of a file server for tests, etc.
- Frameworks and internal software infrastructure available to achieve the project.
- And most importantly, a lot of communication with all team members to clarify the requirements and documents.

It is common in these types of projects that at least one of the participants shares a flowchart to understand the workflow of the entire process.

Auxiliary Diagrams

The following flow chart shows a step-by-step approach to solving the B2B integration project. This auxiliary diagram supports the conversations carried out during the requirements analysis stage.

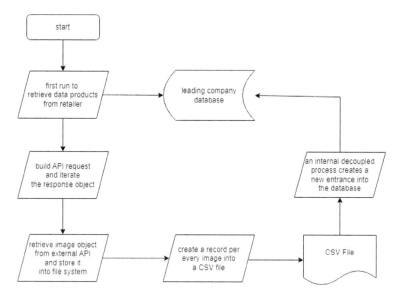

Domain Model

The domain modeling process creates a group of relevant concepts of an area of interest - Domain - that help us solve a specific business problem. The result is a Domain Model.

We already have a domain model in our B2B integration project and will use only the Product entity. Still, we must define which database functions to build to retrieve the data to accomplish our task.

Once you understand the requirements and documentation, the software design principles can help you organize your ideas and build the first effort of your software design.

From Divide and Conquer principle:

- We can define a subtask to handle all the complexities of requests and responses to the external API server. It can be achieved by creating an API client module.

- We can define a sub-task to handle the I-O subroutines to create and read files.

Communicating software design decisions

Once you've talked to your fellow developers, database manager, application server manager, retailer partner, and IT lead, and read the API documentation, emails, and requirements with more detail, you will have an overview of your design proposal.

But you need an effective way to communicate your software design decisions to an external company. We use the C4 model.

Visualizing software architecture

The C4[8] model enables software development teams to describe and communicate software design decisions, similar to Google maps zooming in and out of an area of interest.

These areas of interest in the software are:

Context -> Containers -> Components -> Code - UML Notation

Context diagram

A system context diagram shows the big picture. This diagram shows actors and software systems rather than technologies. For our scenario, it says that building a new web application will achieve the user requirement.

The following abstractions describe the static structure of a context diagram.

Person. A person is a user of your software system. We build a software system to deliver value to a user.

Software System. It describes something that offers value to users. On them, we can execute specific tasks.

---

[8] https://c4model.com/

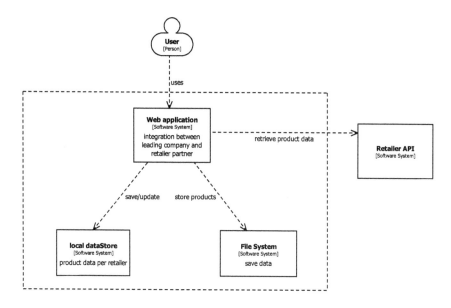

From the diagram above, the retailer can understand that the leading company wants to retrieve product data through a web application. It is irrelevant to them whether the leading company uses a python or java client.

The leading company (dashed lines) may realize that once the product data is retrieved, it is stored on a file server, and a database entry is created.

And what about the front end?

For the design proposal, the front end is irrelevant because once an entry to the database is created, the current logic in the front end retrieves the respective image object from the file server and renders it into a web page.

During the testing stage, we must check the correspondent image object is rendered.

A software system comprises applications and data stores deployed in containers.

Container diagram

Container. A container is something that must be running for an application or data store to work.

Each container is a runtime environment that (not always) runs in its own process space. Inter-container communication takes the form of inter-process communication.

The container diagram shows how the responsibilities of a software system are distributed in different execution units - containers.

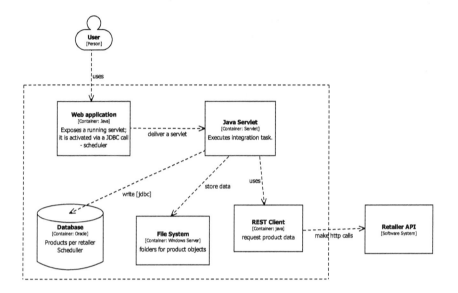

When the web application is deployed to an application server, a servlet waits for a request parameter to start the process, then delegates the task of retrieving data from an external API to a REST client.

The integration process must communicate with a database container such as Oracle to read/write data products and a file system container such as Windows Server to store image objects.

Component diagram

Component. A component is a group of related functionalities encapsulated behind a well-defined interface.

As software designers, we delegate responsibilities to software elements called components that execute sub-tasks with specific technologies to achieve the user software requirements.

The web application executes different groups of related subtasks. For each group of associated subtasks, we define a service. So a component can include many services to achieve its overall goal.

Use the single responsibility and open-closed principles to identify and group these subtasks into single, well-defined services.

The Web application interacts with the user's requests. Then, delegates the execution of different subtasks to three other services.

- *RestClientService* interacts with retailer API to retrieve external product data.
- *FileSystemService* stores these product data on application server folders
- *DataBaseService* reads and writes product data from a local database.

We need to introduce a high-level component called *IntregrationService* that controls the data flow between these services.

Well, you may be tempted to introduce more services, but if they don't add value and support the solution to your business problem, don't. Remember the KISS principle.

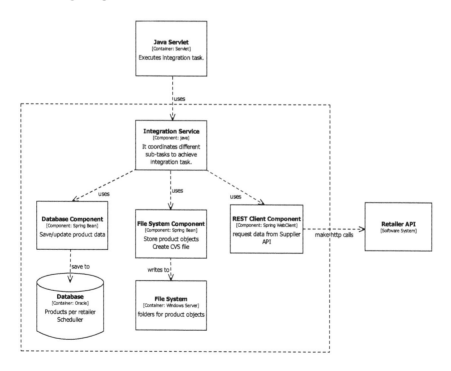

The requirements analysis is not definitive. Change requirements are proportional to the complexity of the project. Or simply because our end users are creative in developing new business ways.

Software design is always an iterative process; when the change requirement comes, it could be the time to identify and introduce new services.

But I think you already got the idea; following software design principles from the beginning of your project; you are building a firewall to protect your code against uncertain change requirements.

Database component

You need to communicate your requirements with the DBA person to implement the required database functionalities to support your integration tasks. There are different formats, for example:

Description

A new database function is required to retrieve product data by retailer.

Parameter

RETAILER_ID	int	ID Retailer

ResultSet

RETAILER_ID	Int	ID Retailer
PRODUCT_ID	Int	ID Product
NAME	String	Product name
PRICE	Double	Product price
DESCRIPTION	String	Product description
VALIDFROM	Date	Product valid from
VALIDUNTIL	Date	Proeuct valid until

Once DBA finishes implementing the database functions, you will receive a set of parameter classes to interact with data.

Code diagram

Finally, we must communicate to the programming factory how each component or module will be implemented as code using UML class diagrams.

From the diagram below, we are telling the programming factory that the *IntegrationService* is the top-level module that needs three dependencies to accomplish its task.

To use dependency injection, we need to target interfaces. Thinking in abstraction, indirectly, we are applying the open-closed principle.

The interface segregation principle recommends including only the methods our application needs to achieve its goals.

Let's see how our class diagram looks. Of course, these services include more methods, but I have decided to include only a few methods for learning purposes.

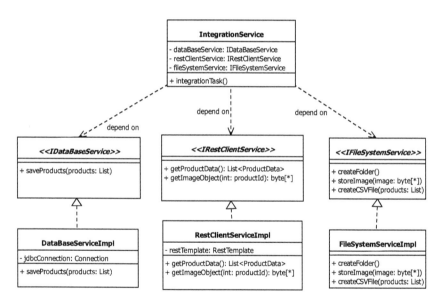

If you see that one of your services needs an additional method because it might be required in the near future, don't include it. Wait until that moment happens. Remember the YAGNI principle.

The *IntegrationService* high-level component is decoupled from its dependencies. When a change occurs in one of its dependencies, there is no impact on the high-level code.

For example, in *RestClientServiceImpl* you want to use the new *WebClient* library to interact with the external API, your code should generate the same *List<ProductData>* object when the *IntegrationService* calls the *getProductData()* method through the interface. High-level modules don't care how the implementation classes are coded. It must respect the contract defined in the interface.

Finally, every component or module in software design is essential to achieve your software product' global goal as a unified whole.

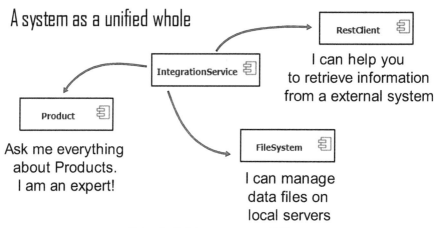

Every module has one responsibility

When you are in charge of software design, remember to think about modularization.

How the new design handle complexity better

Change requirement is under control thanks to abstractions because we know where we need to touch the code in the software.

The cognitive load is minimal because developers do not need to know too much detail about how a method works described in an abstract interface. A developer can understand how the code works and what is needed to make a change thanks to design principles.

There is no duplicated business knowledge in the code because we have delegated specific responsibilities to specific reusable modules.

Dependencies between components are minimal and easy to recognize by using abstractions.

Conclusions

- Loose coupling and High cohesion help reduce dependencies and prepare your code when new changes arrive.

- Minimize external third-party dependencies. These dependencies include excellent methods in their libraries that you can import and reuse. But if your project counts enough resources to implement this in-house method, then do it.

- The software is fragile and very complex. Modularization will be one of your tools to reduce the complexity. Modular code is easier to maintain and refactor.

- The composition should be preferred to inheritance. A design by composition is more flexible to changes than changing a complex chain of Inheritance.

- Any software design is generally a matter of opinion. There is no definitive Guide.

Improving your abstraction ability to model complex business contexts

Improving your abstraction ability to model complex business contexts requires a combination of focused effort, continuous learning, and practical experience. Here are some strategies you can adopt:

- Understand the Business Domain: Gain a deep understanding of the specific business domain you are working in. Familiarize yourself with industry terminology, processes, and key concepts.

- Identify Key Stakeholders: Identify and engage with key stakeholders from different departments or roles within the organization. Understanding their perspectives and requirements is crucial for creating accurate abstractions.

- Ask Questions: Don't hesitate to ask questions to clarify any uncertainties. Engage in discussions with domain experts and stakeholders to gather insights and ensure a comprehensive understanding of the business context.

- Create and refine domain-specific languages (DSLs): Develop DSLs tailored to the specific business domain to bridge the gap between technical and business perspectives. These DSLs provide a more intuitive and domain-specific language for developers to interact with the business concepts.

- Use Visual Tools: Utilize visual tools such as diagrams, flowcharts, and mind maps to represent complex business processes and structures. Visualizations can help in simplifying and clarifying abstract concepts.

- Practice Conceptual Modeling: Practice creating conceptual models that represent the high-level structure and relationships within a business domain. This could include entity-relationship diagrams, use case diagrams, and other modeling techniques.

- Learn Modeling Languages: Familiarize yourself with modeling languages commonly used in business analysis, such as Unified Modeling Language (UML). Understanding these languages can help you express and communicate abstract concepts effectively.

- Break Down Complexity: Break down complex business processes into smaller, more manageable components. This allows you to focus on understanding and abstracting each component individually before considering their interactions.

- Practice regular abstraction exercises: Engage in regular abstraction exercises to hone your ability to identify core concepts, eliminate irrelevant details, and focus on the essence of the business context. These exercises can involve summarizing complex business scenarios, creating concise descriptions of business processes, or identifying patterns in data.

- Seek feedback and mentorship: Seek guidance and feedback from experienced developers and domain experts. Engage in mentorship programs, participate in coding challenges, and seek constructive criticism to identify areas for improvement and refine your abstraction skills.

- Document and Communicate: Document your models and abstractions, and use them as communication tools. Clear documentation helps others understand your abstractions and can serve as a reference for future discussions.

- Stay Updated: Stay informed about changes in the business environment, industry trends, and evolving technologies. This awareness helps you adapt your abstractions to reflect current and future states of the business.

- Collaborate with Others: Collaborate with colleagues, domain experts, and stakeholders. Different perspectives can contribute to a more comprehensive understanding of the business, leading to better abstractions.

- Learn from Experience: Reflect on past projects and experiences. Consider how well your abstractions worked and identify areas for improvement. Learning from practical experience is valuable for refining your abstraction skills.

- Continuous Learning: Stay committed to continuous learning. Attend workshops, training programs, and conferences related to business analysis, modeling, and abstraction. This will help you stay updated on best practices and new methodologies.

www.ingramcontent.com/pod-product-compliance
Lightning Source LLC
LaVergne TN
LVHW051655050326
832903LV00032B/3817